The Other Ladies
of Myanmar

The Other Ladies of Myanmar

Jennifer Rigby

 YUSOF ISHAK INSTITUTE

Published in Singapore in 2018 by
ISEAS Publishing
30 Heng Mui Keng Terrace
Singapore 119614
E-mail: publish@iseas.edu.sg
Website: <http://bookshop.iseas.edu.sg>

The responsibility for facts and opinions in this publication rests exclusively with the author and her interpretations do not necessarily reflect the views or the policy of the publisher or its supporters.

ISEAS Library Cataloguing-in-Publication Data

Rigby, Jennifer.
    1. The Other Ladies of Myanmar.
    2. Women—Myanmar—Social condition.
    3. Women's rights—Myanmar.
    I. Title.
HQ1735.7 R54   May 2018

ISBN 978-981-4818-25-4 (soft cover)
ISBN 978-981-4818-26-1 (ebook, PDF)

Photos on book cover courtesy of David Doyle.

Typeset by Superskill Graphics Pte Ltd
Printed in Singapore by Markono Print Media Pte Ltd

To the Ds, and the other letters in my life
who make my words

Table of Contents

Preface   ix

Acknowledgements   xii

Introduction   xiii

Timeline   xv

1. The Activist: Cheery Zahau   1

2. The Feminist Buddhist Nun: Ketu Mala   14

3. The Survivor: Mi Mi   24

4. The Businesswoman: Yin Myo Su   33

5. The Environmental Campaigner and Princess: Devi Thant Cin   47

6. The Artist: Ma Ei   59

7. The Refugee Sexual Health Nurse: Mu Tha Paw   67

8. The Rohingya and Human Rights Champion: Wai Wai Nu   74

9. The Farmer: Mar Mar Swe   92

10. The Pop Star: Ah Moon   98

11. The Politician: Htin Htin Htay   108

12. The Archer: Aung Ngeain   117

Conclusion   124

About the Author   127

Preface

When I first started thinking about this book in 2015, it was a few months after the first openly contested elections in Myanmar in decades.

After years of oppression and brutality, the political party of democracy hero Aung San Suu Kyi had swept to power, and hope was everywhere.

In the run up to the vote, it had been the word on everyone's lips as I travelled across the country for my work as a journalist. On the night of the election, it rippled through the singing, dancing crowds on the streets of the country's biggest city, Yangon. And it dominated headlines for days afterwards, nationally and globally: the beginnings of hope, freedom and democracy for a people who had lived crushed under military rule for nearly fifty years.

Much of that hope centred on one remarkable woman: Aung San Suu Kyi herself.

She had been a lightning rod for Burmese hope since 1988, when her trip back to her homeland to care for her sick mother coincided with a national democratic uprising that Suu Kyi — the daughter of Burmese independence hero General Aung San — ended up leading.

The 1988 uprising was brutally suppressed, and the military regained control once more. But Suu Kyi did not give up, despite the fact that her efforts to bring freedom to her country saw her incarcerated in some form or another for the majority of the next twenty years.

Her sacrifices, her courage, and her commitment to peaceful protest in the face of oppression made her an icon both at home and abroad. In 1991, she was awarded the Nobel Peace Prize. In Myanmar, she became known as "The Lady", an honorific nickname that gives an indication of her place in the popular imagination of her country.

So it is no surprise that hope was the order of the day on 8 November 2015, as voting slip after voting slip came in backing her party, the National League for Democracy. But now, as I sit down to write this preface two years on, the story is altogether more complicated.

Of course, for anyone to live up to this kind of hope would be near impossible. And for many Burmese people, Suu Kyi is still as much of a hero as she ever was. It is also fair to say that Myanmar is almost unrecognizable from the country it was during the dark days of the military junta, when it was an international pariah cut off from the world, its people living in fear — although the credit for beginning this transformation process has to go to the military-backed civilian government that took over in 2011 (elections were held in 2010 but parliament convened in 2011).

Many challenges remain in Myanmar, from the economy to the environment. But Suu Kyi's approach to these challenges is not the reason why so many — outside Myanmar at least — feel that their hope in her has all but died.

Instead, it is her apparent abandonment of the values she was once believed to embody in the case of one particular group of Burmese citizens, the Rohingya. An unimaginably horrific campaign of violence, meted out by the still-powerful Burmese army against this group in recent months, has seen around 700,000 flee, as the world wakes up to the fact that Suu Kyi's government is looking the other way while at least ethnic cleansing, and possibly even genocide, takes place in Myanmar.

And it is worse than just looking away: the government has actively denied reports of atrocities, denied access to observers and aid, and even called some Rohingya "terrorists" (there are insurgent groups within the community).

This approach has played well in Myanmar, where many are united over the belief that the Rohingya are dangerous illegal immigrants. Others in the country say Suu Kyi is on a knife-edge, effectively sacrificing the few for the many in the face of the army's thirst for blood (or the fear that the generals could once more take total control of Myanmar).

But for a human rights icon to so blatantly ignore the human rights of an entire ethnic group has poisoned the hope the world had in Suu

Kyi. However the current crisis is resolved, the story of Myanmar will never be the fairy-tale democratic transition that many (perhaps naively) thought it could be.

When I set out to write this book, I listened to the Burmese people I met, and I too had hope in Suu Kyi. But her struggle was so widely covered, her story so completely known, that I didn't feel I could add anything to that particular story of hope.

Instead, ironically, I also listened to Suu Kyi herself. In the days before the election, at a baking hot rally in Yangon that I attended, she told the heaving crowd that democracy was about hope and belief in the people themselves.

"That's why I'm not afraid at all," she told tens of thousands of her supporters. "Because I believe in you."

It was inspiring, and I was inspired, and I started thinking about all the other people in Myanmar who had been working for this moment for their whole lives, and in whose hands Suu Kyi herself believed a democratic future rested.

So I decided to write about these other people in Myanmar who would shape their country in the coming years. Specifically, I decided to write about the women — the "Other Ladies" of the title — partly because of my own journalistic interest in women's rights, but also because I felt that their voices had been the least heard in the story of Myanmar thus far.

Their voices are what you are about to read. I hope you enjoy hearing them.

Acknowledgements

My greatest thanks go to the twelve wonderful women who opened their lives to me so warmly and graciously, and allowed me to tell their stories. Then also to my friend Thal Nyein Thu (Grace), who helped inspire the book (she's quite the lady herself), as well as always being there to help with translation. Thanks are also due to all of the translators I worked with, as well as the organizations who helped me reach the women I spoke to; a particular shout-out to the Tavoy Women's Union, who took this quite literally and gave me a backy on their motorbikes into the jungle to meet Htin Htin Htay. And finally to the International Women's Media Foundation, who funded the research.

Introduction

I have a fantastic old Burmese cookbook on my bookshelves, which proudly informs me that there is no need for feminism in Myanmar.

Great stuff, I think. Things must be totally equal here. So, why's that, then? Ah. Hang on.

There is no need for feminism, I learn, "because it is every Burmese woman's sole aim to become a wife."

The situation for women in Myanmar is actually even more complicated, and multifaceted, than this suggests. Take the country's 2008 constitution. While article 348 proclaims: "The Union shall not discriminate any citizen of the Republic of the Union of Myanmar, based on race, birth, religion, official position, status, culture, sex and wealth", elsewhere, some government jobs are described as being "naturally suitable for men only".

While Aung San Suu Kyi is currently the country's de facto leader, she first rose to prominence thanks to her famous father, the country's independence hero General Aung San.

While the country is 80th out of 159 countries in the United Nations' most recent gender equality index, it is higher than many of its neighbours: Cambodia (112), Laos (106), and even India (125).

And looking at the situation in the past does not clear things up much, either. There is an amazing article in *The Atlantic* from 1958 by Mya Sein, former head of the Burma Women's Council. It recounts how she was surprised by how fiercely the British colonialists fought back against attempts by the more emancipated Burmese women to get some female representation in the Legislature in 1927.

The backward Brits didn't hold out, though; the first Burmese woman was elected in 1929. But some would argue the situation since then has gone backwards. As the country unravelled in the hands of the generals in the latter half of the twentieth century, women's rights took a similar nosedive.

As such, there are still effectively no laws protecting women from domestic violence, and rape is routinely used as a weapon of war in regional ethnic conflicts. In some rural areas, women have no inheritance rights, no sexual education, and no access to contraception.

But things are changing. As I have already explained, while the election of Suu Kyi has not been a silver bullet, Myanmar is undoubtedly in the process of developing, transforming, and opening up to the world.

As such, the situation for its women has come under increased scrutiny, both from outside the country but also from the women within it.

Some of these clued-up Burmese gender campaigners are featured in this book, but it is not exclusively about them, because they do not represent the majority of women in this largely rural and extremely poor society. Instead, I have tried to speak to and write about women who represent different elements of Myanmar, and whose stories offer insights into some of the challenges both women and men are facing across the country as it develops and changes.

That means the women I have spoken to include a farmer and a refugee as well as a pop star and a nun. Their stories illuminate different areas of Burmese life, whether that is religious life, cultural life, or something else entirely — and sometimes, life or death.

In short, this book aims to tell the fascinating and fluctuating story of Myanmar and the changes it is currently experiencing through the voices of its women.

From the artist who defied the junta to hand out sanitary towels to guests at her exhibition, to the pop star who gets called a whore for wearing short skirts; from the young Muslim campaigner who has already spent a quarter of her life in prison, to the refugee who learned how to give her sisters the contraceptive implant in a refugee camp; these are the voices of The Other Ladies of Myanmar.

Timeline

This book is about Myanmar's present and its future, but the past is important, too.

With that in mind, here is a short orientation paragraph and a brief timeline of key events in the country's recent history that are either mentioned in this book, or are relevant to *The Other Ladies of Myanmar*.

First some basics: Myanmar, also known as Burma (see the note at the end of this section) is a country in Southeast Asia housing around 53 million people. Its population is made up of more than 100 ethnic groups, although its majority religion is Buddhism. It is bordered by Bangladesh, India, China, Laos, and Thailand.

1885: Colonial takeover

In 1885, the United Kingdom completed its takeover of the Burmese kingdom, and exiled its royal family.

1947: War, Burmese independence and tragedy

The beginning of the end for British rule in Burma. Following the Second World War, in which Burma became a battleground between the Japanese and the Allies, calls for Burmese independence grew.

Aung San Suu Kyi's father, General Aung San, orchestrated the country's freedom from colonial rule, followed by the drive to unite many of Burma's different ethnicities in the new union via the Panglong agreement.

Tragically, after winning a landslide election in April 1947, Aung San and six of his colleagues were assassinated in a council chamber in Yangon (then known as Rangoon).

1948: Officially free — but fighting

On 4 January 1948, Burma officially got its independence. But without charismatic Aung San, the country slid into political instability, civil war and conflict — between the new Burmese army and the Communists as well as with a number of ethnic groups.

1962: The military coup d'état

By 1962, the fearsome Burmese army (known as the Tatmadaw) tired of doing what it was told by the civilian government, and seized power in a coup.

General Ne Win immediately embarked on the Burmese Way to Socialism, a disastrous programme that wrecked the country's economy and isolated it from the world.

1988: The 8888 uprising

Protests against the increasingly brutal regime took place throughout the following decades. But the 1988 demonstrations, which ignited a generation and spread across the country, were the largest, and forced the resignation of Ne Win (after he warned the army would "shoot to kill" if more protests took place — which it did).

Meanwhile, Aung San Suu Kyi returned to Myanmar. She had been living in England but came back to care for her sick mother. She joined the protests and ultimately, via her first public speech in Yangon to half a million people, became the symbol of freedom and democracy for a nation.

But despite Ne Win's resignation, little changed; the generals reorganized and renamed the ruling party, becoming the fearsome State Law and Order Restoration Council (SLORC).

1990: The ignored elections

After huge international and national pressure, the junta arranged the first "free" elections in Myanmar for thirty years in May 1990. Suu Kyi's National League for Democracy (NLD) won a landslide victory in the poll, and so the regime promptly ignored it.

In 1992, General Than Shwe took over as leader of SLORC and became effectively the country's second dictatorial leader.

Suu Kyi was placed under house arrest shortly after the election (other NLD figures were also imprisoned), and would spend fifteen of the next twenty-one years there, advocating for non-violent protest and democracy but unable to see her sons or even her sick husband, who died of cancer in England in 1999. In 1991 she won the Nobel Peace Prize for her struggle.

2007: The Saffron Revolution

Monks, highly respected figures in Myanmar, backed major protests against fuel price rises and the wider regime. But things ended in the now-familiar way: horrifying violence, a brutal crackdown by the regime, and little other change for ordinary Burmese people. At least this time the world was watching, as reporters managed to smuggle out tapes.

2008: Cyclone Nargis

The devastating effects of this huge tropical storm — which slammed into the Irrawaddy Delta region on 2 May 2008 — were exacerbated by the military regime's refusal to let foreign aid enter the country in the aftermath.

Hundreds of thousands died and 700,000 homes were destroyed. The aid ban was eventually lifted, but by then many more had died. The total death toll is unknown but the UN estimates that up to 2.4 million people were affected in some way by Myanmar's worst ever natural disaster.

2010: All change? The path to democracy

More "free" elections for Myanmar took place in November 2010, and this time the NLD were effectively barred from taking part. Unsurprisingly, the military-backed Union Solidarity and Development Party (USDP) won amid reports of vote-rigging.

But there were positives. While the generals remained at the elbows of the USDP, the government was now at least nominally civilian. Led by President Thein Sein (himself a former general), it embarked on a series of reforms which surprised many — not least allowing the release of Suu Kyi from house arrest later that month (her party was even allowed to compete in 2012 by-elections, in which The Lady won a seat).

Over the next few years, some political prisoners were freed, censorship was slightly relaxed, and a peace treaty with at least some ethnic combatants was signed. The changes were enough for some international sanctions to be lifted — and hope for a better future began to flower in Myanmar.

2015 Landmark elections and hopes for the future

That hope bore shining fruit in November 2015, when Suu Kyi's NLD party won a landslide victory in national elections that were considerably closer to actually being free and fair than many had hoped — albeit still not perfect.

Inevitably, the real world has since been a bit more complicated: the military still controls 25 per cent of the seats in parliament, and the constitution blocked Suu Kyi from becoming president (instead, her ally Win Myint (as of March 2018) is in the seat and she is in the newly created "state counsellor" role).

But there are wider concerns. A new wave of violence against the Rohingya Muslim minority has been dismissed by Suu Kyi, despite international condemnation that the army's treatment may amount to ethnic cleansing or even genocide; curbs on freedom of speech and convictions for defamation have crept up; ethnic conflicts continue; and there have been no real reforms aimed at tackling the crippling poverty that most Burmese still face — indeed, a vague economic plan means foreign investment is likely to fall.

It cannot all be blamed on Suu Kyi, still lovingly known as "The Lady" in Myanmar; but whether that fruit of hope that seemed so ripe in 2015 will be harvested, or whether it withers on the vine, is effectively in her hands.

Burma or Myanmar?

Finally, a note on the name of the country.

What's in a name? In Burma/Myanmar, at least until recently, a lot. Burma was renamed as Myanmar by the military junta in 1989, who said they were rejecting the old colonial name of "Burma" and seizing the country back for its people.

While historians generally reject this interpretation anyway — most agree that the words are basically very similar in Burmese, with Myanmar the more literary or historical form, and Burma the more colloquial — it caused the international community serious confusion.

Aung San Suu Kyi stuck with Burma, saying that to do anything else would be to give the new name, and hence the military regime, legitimacy. Allies like the United States and United Kingdom did the same, but the UN went with Myanmar. Even today, it is confusing. For example, while you land in Yangon International Airport, your luggage tags are stamped "RGN" for Rangoon, the city's Myanmar/Burma equivalents.

Nowadays though, with the wider changes and challenges in the country, the issues is less fraught. Many Burmese use Myanmar, or the two names interchangeably, and diplomats — including Suu Kyi herself — are more open to compromise.

As such, I will mainly use "Myanmar" but Burma also slips in, particularly when I am speaking about historical events or indeed if the women themselves use Burma.

CHAPTER ONE

The Activist: Cheery Zahau

WHEN I first meet Cheery Zahau, she's pregnant with her first child, and so am I. She's about one month further along than me, and we share a little whine about morning sickness before she reassures me that it will get better soon, which is a lifeline I cling to for some time. I feel sheepish because while she had morning sickness, she travelled Myanmar interviewing youth groups and rape survivors, while I mainly stayed in my flat in the air conditioning, eating my way out of the nausea.

There's another coincidence too: both of our sisters are also pregnant. But that's where the similarities end, because a few months after we meet, her sister gives birth.

Her baby is healthy, but her experience is horrible, and it stems from the racism in Myanmar that Cheery has been fighting against her whole life. Cheery and her family are Chin, an ethnic group from the north of the country. Her people are no longer at war with the Burmese government, but they have been widely discriminated against for decades, and their region remains amongst the poorest and most neglected in a country where there is stiff competition for that miserable crown.

Cheery's sister had her baby in Yangon, where Cheery's family now live. First of all, the electricity went out, leaving her sister to deliver by torchlight for two hours. She was bleeding too much, cold and frightened, but there were no doctors to help. When Cheery went to find some doctors, she was told: "You Chin people, you all come in the labour room, are you bringing your whole nation here? You can't be here, get out."

The next intervention from a medical professional came from a nurse, shouting: "Where is that Chin?" and handing Cheery a file. Hours later, when she was trying to stay because her sister (who speaks Chin but not Burmese) needed an interpreter, Cheery was told: "This hospital is not for those who can't speak."

Cheery, shocked by the whole experience, wrote online: "Because of this type of people, I am disgusted [by] this country."

It's a reminder of the everyday barriers to life faced by Cheery and her people. After decades of isolation and chronic lack of funds, the health service across Myanmar doesn't have the best of reputations for anyone, but at least most patients would not have to face out-and-out discrimination as well, while at their most vulnerable.

Throughout our conversations, Cheery tells me stories like this — not just about her family, and not just about Chin people, either. Her work is in human rights, and she has fought for all of the ethnicities of Myanmar, and particularly for women, to be treated better for her whole life.

It's a fight that has often put her in danger. She has been chased around the countryside by Myanmar's fearsome military (known as the Tatmadaw) at a time when, as the rulers of the country in previous decades, they had absolute impunity.

Cheery says she doesn't know when she realized that she was going to have a life like this. But as we meet up and talk over several months, I realize that she was fighting for others even as a little girl growing up in a remote village in Sagaing region.

"We lived in the north part of the village, and the pharmacy is in the south part. Whenever the children are sick, the mothers came to me and asked me to buy the medicine for their children," she says. "At the time, I thought, this is so unfair! They have their own kids! But," she pauses. "I have to do it."

Cheery's family were a poor family living in a poor region. Her father fled to Mizoram, a border state in India, in 1989, the year after Myanmar's military junta crushed the famous 1988 democratic uprising that had Aung San Suu Kyi as its figurehead. Her mother left a few years later, so Cheery was brought up by her grandmother.

Aged eleven, she was sent to boarding school 14 miles away from her home village of Kalaymyo. Her school was Christian because most

Chin people are also Christian — they converted after missionaries from Britain and other countries came to their region, mainly in the second half of the nineteenth century.

When Cheery went to school in the 1990s, there were no motorbikes, cars or buses in her area. The only vehicle was a pushbike. So, once a month, Cheery cycled back to see her grandmother. It took her a whole day.

At home, she was responsible for helping her grandmother on the family farm, gathering crabs and fish from the rice fields, cleaning up and, (according to Cheery), slightly resentfully doing more than her sister or uncle, who were a similar age and lived with the family.

In between, in an enterprising fashion for an eleven-year-old, she used to cycle over to a nearby market and buy snacks to sell to her fellow kids.

"I don't normally tell this story — it's embarrassing — but when my flip flop was torn apart, I'd go door to door selling my snacks, and I'd always make double. I have to make money myself. Now I realize I was an entrepreneur! I can buy my flip flops, and I don't need to rely on money from my parents," she says.

Her responsibilities didn't lessen at school, where — thanks to an astute teacher who could clearly recognize leadership potential when she saw it — she was put in charge of the girl's dorm, responsible for making her fellow pupils get up at 5.30 a.m. for breakfast and devotion.

Experiences like this in Cheery's schooldays shaped her, and so did the textbooks she was supposed to read.

"In the textbooks, it suggests we are backward people, and we are not. We are just poor. It also suggests the Shan people [another ethnicity] are bad because they do drugs, the Kachin people are bad because they want their own state.

"So all these norms about people, we learn in the text books — and of course, the Bamar [the dominant ethnicity, which Aung San Suu Kyi belongs to] are superior," says Cheery.

But she was never the kind of child who would take this lying down. In fact, her innocent questions at a time of great oppression in Myanmar

— Cheery grew up while the country was ruled by the military junta, which was in power from 1962 to 2011 — led her teachers to describe her as having "one foot in prison".

When she finished high school, aged seventeen, her teachers warned her not to go to university in Myanmar because of the risk that her outspokenness and leadership potential would be punished.

"They all said, you will be in trouble. They knew I was going to organize something, and I would have ended up in jail," says Cheery.

Mindful of their advice, she instead joined her parents in Mizoram, India, hoping for further study as well as some political experience and volunteering. But she was immediately faced with discrimination.

"They always call me smelly, fish paste [fermented fish paste is a popular — and odorous — ingredient in Burmese cooking]. There was lots of discrimination," says Cheery.

It was a taster of the events of 2003, which would change Cheery's life forever and shape her determination to make a difference in an unfeeling, unfair world.

In July 2003, there was a rape case where a Burmese man was accused of raping a Mizo girl of around fourteen years old. There was a lot of misinformation about the case, and some say the perpetrator was actually her Indian neighbour, but it was too late: the damage to the image of the Burmese refugees was done.

Soon, the biggest organizations in Mizoram state began broadcasting how all Burmese people were bad, drug dealers and rapists, and should leave. Then, every village and town in the state began running loudspeaker announcements saying all Burmese must get out.

"It was terrifying. So that was July, in heavy monsoon rain. I was working with a women's organization, and suddenly we have lots and lots of women and children coming to our office and asking to stay, to take shelter," says Cheery.

Landlords had started evicting Burmese people, and in some areas even throwing their belongings out on the street.

"There was terrible, terrible violence. One Mizo politician kindly allowed us to use his empty house so we spread the word that people can take shelter there. Women came to us telling us people had chased them away with iron sticks," she says.

Cheery headed out to document the violence being done to her people.

"It was so crazy. We were exhausted, and we could not even go home. My parents were hiding. I was hiding. We were hiding for four months ... it's something that is difficult for me to talk about. Sometimes I just skip this part when I talk to journalists, because it's too crazy. The fear in those four months, I cannot even express it," she remembers.

By November, things calmed down after a lot of pressure on the Indian government and the regional Mizoram government.

"But before that, about 20,000 people were deported, some died on the way to Chin state, some delivered babies on the way, some caught malaria. And the people who stayed in Mizoram were the ones who cannot go back to Burma because they have problems with the military there, or no one to turn to on the Burma side. It was a nightmare," says Cheery [she uses the old name for Myanmar, Burma, when talking about her country].

"But in the middle of the crisis, there are always good people. Our landlord was kind, he locked us in from the outside, so when people came it looked like the house was empty but we were inside, working with the women. It sounds like the Jewish and the Nazis right? It was crazy."

It also sounds to me like the definitive end of innocence for Cheery, who was twenty-two years old at the time. But she says it was also a beginning.

"So one day I was praying — I mean, complaining really — because we tried to contact human rights groups and the only two who gave us a response were Amnesty and Refugee International.

So I was upset and tired and very frightened, and I complained to God: 'We cannot live in Burma because of the military oppression and we come here, my Chin people come here, and they still face this. And the international community does not know us, the Burmese community does not know us, so — why did you create people like us who will be mistreated like this?'"

Then, she heard a voice.

"This voice came in. 'It is your job to speak,' it said. And that's that," says Cheery. Whether the voice was God or her own inner leader piping up, the decision was made: her life would be dedicated to activism, and to others.

That voice has motivated her ever since to try and make a difference, often at great personal risk.

Cheery is probably most famous in Myanmar for her work on the military using rape as a weapon of war against the Chin people.

In 2007, with her team from the Women's League of Chinland, she documented thirty-eight cases of the military raping Chin women. It was a number that Cheery described at the time as the tip of the iceberg.

The Chins are not the only ethnicity to have suffered in this way in the past few decades in Myanmar: numerous credible reports have found that the Burmese military has used rape as a weapon of war and oppression for years against many different ethnic minorities, from Kachin women to Mon women. In fact, as I write, there are reports that the same thing is going on now — under Aung San Suu Kyi's government — with thirty Muslim women seemingly raped by soldiers in a flare-up of violence in Rakhine State in a single afternoon in October 2016. The reports are difficult to verify because no foreign reporters are allowed into the region.

Nearly 2,000 women have come forward about military rape in Myanmar, but the risks associated with doing so mean that the likely total affected is much, much higher. In Cheery's report, the youngest girl targeted was twelve, and almost half were gang-raped.

At the time, Cheery wrote: "In one case, a woman was stripped naked and hung on a cross, in a deliberate act of mockery against her Christian religion. This indicates that sexual violence is being deliberately used as a weapon to torture and terrorize local ethnic populations into submission. There is a collective understanding among the troops that they can rape with impunity."

No one was ever prosecuted for the rapes, and women who complained were threatened. So were Cheery and her team.

"When you investigate rape by the security forces or the government army, you are under threat. Those guys are untouchable," she says.

She points out that the entire process, which took place over several months in 2006, was incredibly risky — mainly for the victims and for her team in the field.

"The army were looking for us all over the place. We had to do it quietly and quickly. Sometimes we travelled at 4 o'clock in the morning because we know that the army is in another village just four miles away, so we have to run away," she says quietly.

Cheery says her team took the most risks, as she spent time in the office coordinating efforts while they were almost entirely on the ground in Myanmar, where at that time there were thirteen army battalions stationed across thirty-three military outposts in the area.

"Sometimes we are missing some info because the researchers could not have paper, for security reasons, so they had to remember," she says.

I ask her if she was ever frightened, and she laughs a bit at her own youthful bravery.

"Actually, no," she responds. "I would be now, but I was so young. When I started the Women's League of Chinland, I was twenty-three. I don't know how I pulled this off. But I was so young, so naive, so full of commitment to document what was happening to Chin people that I didn't look at what might happen to me."

The release of the report in New Delhi on 27 March 2007 — Tatmadaw Day — was like a bomb going off for the international community. Although in Myanmar, organizations were queuing up to denounce Cheery and her report, the world was beginning to pay attention.

In the weeks before the release, Cheery was asked to testify about military rape in Myanmar at the UN, as well as to meet officials in London and Brussels.

"This was the first time they ever heard about the Chin situation," she says. "I talked about not only Chin but the mass rape across Burma. The room was packed. I was shaking. But when I spoke, you could hear a pin drop. It was silent."

International pressure is, in part, what eventually brought Myanmar to the semi-democratic place it is in now (although as mentioned, military rape is far from a historic horror).

Documenting it back in 2007, though, meant that Cheery had to flee to Thailand, as she was no longer safe even in Mizoram.

"There were a lot of threats. Someone sent me a radio transmission of the Burma army asking the Indian army to arrest me," she says. "Then in 2007, the Burmese military government sent a letter to the defence department in Chin state. They made everyone, especially the women, line up and asked [them] how they are linked to me. 'Where is Cheery Zahau? Are you related to Cheery Zahau? Have you received money from Cheery Zahau? Have you had training from her?'"

Her family were forced to disown her, and people crossing the border were shown her photograph and asked if they'd seen "this girl" — at which point in her story Cheery laughs, and points out that she crossed the border plenty of times herself, but just wasn't seen.

"I was not attacked physically because I was very lucky to escape. Of course, if I had ever been in their [the army's] hands, it would have been finished," she says.

At some point among all of this harassment, Cheery thinks now that she became depressed, particularly after immersing herself so deeply in the testimony of the rape survivors she met.

"What I noticed at the time was that I was drinking too much. I didn't drink until the age of twenty-five, and by the time I did, I was drinking far too much. I was not drinking every day or drinking alone, but [before] I don't drink alcohol, that's just not me. It's not how I grew up. And I didn't trust men, because of what I had heard," she says.

For this reason, alongside the continued persecution, she decided to move to Chiang Mai in Thailand in 2008, long a haven for Burmese dissidents, and "stay quiet" for a few years.

"In Chiang Mai I was out of that hectic situation so I had some private time and I realized I was very angry. I did not realize I was depressed at the time, only after. But once you are upset like that, angry and distrustful, you cannot have a relationship with anybody," she says.

In the end Cheery spent three years there before coming back to Myanmar in 2011, when the military junta handed over power to a military-backed civilian government and the country began to open up to the outside world.

As you would expect, she hasn't kept quiet since. Cheery still fights for human rights, for women and for the Chin people. She represents and amplifies their voices on a national level but also quite literally puts her back into it: physically building roads and bridges in the remote region in the absence of any government support.

She has some good stories about these trips. On one journey, on a pretty hairy-sounding motorbike ride through a landslide (sheeting rain, clinging on, dodging falling rocks) that Cheery realized she needed to pee. I first hear her tell this story at an International Women's Day event in 2016, and she brings the house down by asking "Can I be a bit dirty?" before she continues her story.

The men stopped to let her pee, amid much embarrassment and squirming on their part. It's a jokey tale, but with a serious point. In a conservative society like Myanmar, that's an awkward question to ask, and it's hard to be the woman asking it when some on the trip may well have thought you had no business being there in the first place.

Pee stops aside, Cheery also still opposes the government where necessary, including even standing against Aung San Suu Kyi's NLD party for the local Falam seat in 2015's historic elections.

The campaign against her was a rare dispiriting and dark moment among the general jubilation that greeted Aung San Suu Kyi's historic path to victory. It focused on her support for Myanmar's Rohingya Muslim minority, one of the most persecuted groups in the world (see Chapter 8).

Cheery supports their plight, seeing in it a more extreme version of what the Chin people have experienced. But many Burmese people are anti-Muslim, and Aung San Suu Kyi has not only done nothing since her election to help these people; she has stood by as the situation for them has dramatically worsened.

"I was very disappointed with that campaign. We did not argue on the issues. We argued on false information, and one of the very successful tactics used against me was the Rohingya issue," says Cheery.

"At a youth dinner before the election, some people were talking in a very demeaning way about the Muslims, and of course I had to intervene, right? I can't let people assume all Muslims are terrorists or they don't belong here or they will destroy Chin society."

She said it was one of the moments when her religion helped her to think clearly, regardless of the fact that it might cost her the election.

"At the end of the day, you cannot send people off to sea and let them die in the boat [many Rohingya have attempted the perilous sea crossing to escape Myanmar and find better lives in neighbouring countries like Thailand or Malaysia, and many have died as a result]," she says. "If Jesus was alive, he is not going to do that. Or any God. So we need to find solutions."

Perhaps as a result of her interventions on issues like this, Cheery didn't win, but says she learned lessons and might run again. If she does, it is unlikely to be as a candidate for Aung San Suu Kyi's party. While Cheery admires "The Lady", as she's known in Myanmar, she is concerned that her party is not held up to a high enough standard, because anything is better than the past.

Moreover, she is worried about the ongoing power of the military and their actions in the continuing ethnic conflicts that have flared up in various regions of Myanmar since the election. While the NLD won the election, the military is still incredibly powerful: a quarter of seats in parliament are reserved for military personnel, and as well as its own ongoing autonomy, it also effectively controls the defence, home and border affairs ministries, and also has veto powers.

"And this is the same institution that has done all these human rights violations, restricted activists, and they continue to do so," says Cheery. "It's more and more complicated with the new government. The Tatmadaw has not changed. Even the biggest governments who come to talk, they say bad guys can be good guys. But they don't change so easily."

"I always gave the warning before the election that the NLD combined with the Tatmadaw is a disaster for ethnic people. And that is happening."

One thing she is hopeful about, though, is the changing situation for women in the new Myanmar. "The fact that we can even discuss women's issues is a change from the past, but we still have a long way to go," she says.

She tells me a story about her ID card. As a Burmese woman, the status written on your ID card — if you are either a single woman living with your parents, as most Burmese do before marriage, or if you are married — is "dependant".

"Mei ko ku it is called in Burmese. Ask ten women in this country what is written on their identity card, and it is dependant. So those woman who often have lots of responsibilities are still legally dependants, they have no rights to ownership when they want to get loans, there are a lot of legal barriers," says Cheery.

"Even for someone like me, I have to fight with the authorities — we had a big argument, twice — to change it to private business owner because I have my own thing, my research, my skills. But he kept writing dependant. And I went back to him. Write I am a business owner. Write it. But it's a long battle and a lot of girls won't do that."

For middle and upper class women, there are ways round this, and they are often quite educated and independent, says Cheery. But for poorer women in rural areas, there's a double burden — taking care of the families at the same time as having to make money to survive, and this is not recognized. For Chin women it's even worse, as they take on even more responsibility. If someone gets sick, it is their responsibility to look after that person on top of their work in the family and the field, but they have no access to any inheritance, which goes to the male members of the family by custom.

"The fact that Chin women are very much disempowered in the family makes me want to speak up. And how people treat me, how men treat me. 'Oh this is a young girl, her voice doesn't matter' — I have been told that a lot," she says.

So this inequality on the familial level is next on her agenda. First though, she has to finish her report for the Women's League of Burma. This time, it's about violence and rape in a domestic context, and the women who — in the face of very little state support — help those who try to escape. (See Chapter 3 for more on the lack of provisions for survivors of domestic violence.)

"The last interview was about an infant girl being raped by her neighbour. Two years and eight months old. A baby ... it's sick," she says. "And the only services available are from these women's organizations, but they are limited financially — there's nothing from the government. In some areas the courts are reasonably active. In others, it is disappointing."

She says the experience has made her feel that society is "broken", with unspeakable brutality like this still barely discussed as a result of societal taboos about sex. In many cases, the women who help the survivors become the target of the perpetrators, who tell them things like "I will come out of jail, and I will get you". Or they are told that rape is a private matter that they shouldn't be involved in. Cheery says the experience has made her both sorrowful and proud of the victims and the women helping them.

"These women who help rape survivors, they are the real heroes," she says.

She remembers another woman she met, a Chin woman in Mizoram, in 2008. She had four children, and sold ice cream on the street to provide for them. If she didn't make 20 rupees a day (5,000 Burmese kyat, or less than US$4), she sent her children to neighbours for dinner, and skipped eating herself. At the same time, she was fighting for her children to be included in scholarship programmes to ensure their lives were not as hard as hers has been.

"When I met this woman, I cried a lot, and I still get emotional when I talk about her, because I realize how government inaction can cause extreme poverty, and let this type of situation for women happen," says Cheery.

"So this woman for me is also the real hero, she is my hero, the hero for her children. And I think we don't draw enough strength from other women, ordinary women who do amazing work, who risk their lives for others, who make their society better, their communities better."

I tell Cheery I think she is a hero, and she laughs it off. But she does hope her voice will help amplify others.

"I love the sky," she says, a little dreamily. "But to me, if there's only one star in the sky, it's not pretty, it's not complete. So we need to have lots of stars. In women and politics, we need to have lots of stars, lots of women, championing education, reproductive health, business. That is what I hope for women, and that is our purpose for doing what we do."

CHAPTER TWO

The Feminist Buddhist Nun: Ketu Mala

IN MYANMAR, one of the most common everyday sights is a line of Buddhist monks, barefoot, shaven headed, clad in scarlet robes. Early in the morning, they queue up outside shops, houses and restaurants to receive alms — food and support from lay people.

For foreigners, they are also one of the most exotic sights, eagerly snapped on smartphones and cameras. But you don't just see monks. There are nuns too, also with bare feet and shaven heads. They normally wear pink robes with an orange sash.

However, according to the type of Buddhism practised in Myanmar, they are not really nuns at all. According to Theravada Buddhism, women cannot be ordained as nuns, because their order is basically extinct. They are, at best, known as "renunciants", lay women who have taken vows to live according to Buddha's teachings — and there are 60,000 of them in Myanmar (despite their official non-existence).

But these nuns can't preach, become senior members of the Buddhist community, or even enter some parts of pagodas. They also don't get anywhere near the respect afforded to monks in this deeply religious country, and often even struggle for food donations. It's hardly the image of equality, tolerance and harmony that Buddhism often has in the West.

Ketu Mala is a Burmese nun, and she's not happy about this inequality. She's not just any nun, either. She founded the incredibly successful Dhamma School Foundation, which brings Buddhist teachings into education in Myanmar. She recently met UN Secretary General Ban

Ki-Moon, and leads lectures all over Asia. And she's a feminist — a feminist nun.

We meet in one of her friend's houses near Yangon airport.

"Let's face it," she says, speaking partly in English and partly Burmese. "Myanmar has and has had a male-dominated, patriarchal society, which also means the majority of religion is also dominated by men. The role of women in the religious sector can sometimes even be remarked upon as non-existent. It's that small. Why? Because the patriarchy is deep-rooted in Myanmar, this is the main point."

To even say these kinds of things in Myanmar is pretty incendiary. Ketu Mala explains that the leading monks in Myanmar, known as the Bhikkhu Sangha, find this kind of talk threatening.

"If I am talking to the monks, I have to move wisely and carefully. I would not even sit like this, I have to do it like this," she says, bowing as she speaks. "Some of the monks, they think if I am talking about the gender issue, I am in competition with them. So I don't want that. So I just have to explain to them, this is not to compete with you, the monks, or monk society. This is just for our confidence, for women."

She says the monks are actually afraid of the return of the Bhikkhuni Sangha, the order of nuns, which has effectively died out in Myanmar.

"They don't even want to hear this name," she says. "So for the last two or three years, if I am talking, I can't use this word."

She's wise to be cautious: she tells me the tale of a nun called Thisawaddy, who went to Sri Lanka to become ordained in the Bhikkhuni Sangha order. She came back to Myanmar around the year 2000, when the military government still held the country in its unshakeable fist. She was told she could only return if she changed back to her previous guise. Understandably, she felt she did not want to, or even could not, do this. She was arrested at the airport and imprisoned for six months.

"There was lots of suffering for her, because she became a Bhikkhuni," says Ketu Mala. When she got out of prison, she was sent to the airport and told she could not stay in Myanmar. Heartbreakingly, she later suffered from psychological problems as a result of the beatings and tortures she had undergone in prison, and disrobed five years later.

"So in Myanmar conditions are like this, so it's not easy to talk about gender. They think if I am talking about gender issues, I want to be the king," laughs Ketu Mala. "So it's impossible, and I do not want to try impossible things."

As such, she has given up on the revival of the Bhikkhuni Sangha order in Myanmar, even though it has made a comeback in other Theravada countries, like Sri Lanka and even Thailand — although it is still a contentious issue in the latter. Instead, she is focusing on rehabilitating the image of nuns in the country.

But the really strange thing is that the Bhikkhuni Sangha, or nuns or female monks in general, is not some new-fangled invention designed to upset the natural order. The concept is ancient — as old as Buddha himself.

"In Buddha's time, when he was preaching, on one side there were the male monks, on the other side the female monks. He gave them an equal role," says Ketu Mala.

She's not wrong: while the issue is still debated in Buddhism, it is clear that Buddha created the Bhikkhuni Sangha for his stepmother and aunt, Mahapajapati, after she and 500 other women undertook a pilgrimage to prove themselves.

He is also understood to have said: "Women are equal to men in their potential to achieve enlightenment" — the first leader in any religion to say anything so egalitarian. It's a statement that was almost unthinkable at the time, because in ancient India, where Buddhism began, women very rarely left household life.

But since then, it feels like Buddhism in some countries has gone backwards. Ketu Mala first felt the injustice when she was around thirteen, living near Mawlaymyine in the south of Myanmar. Her uncle and cousin were being ordained as monks. In Myanmar, this is almost like military service. Most young men join the monkhood for a period as part of the process of growing up. Ketu Mala and her family went along to watch, but the women were not allowed into the most sacred place, where the ordination actually happened. A tersely worded signpost prevented their entry.

"So we are waiting outside, and I am thinking why am I not allowed inside? I am so afraid — I am thinking, will I destroy this room?" she says. "I am a schoolgirl and I like to follow rules, but for the first time I am feeling different from the males and I am thinking, why can a man do that, and I cannot?"

She later went on a retreat to Pa-Auk Forest Monastery, about 10 miles from her town. Here, women can go everywhere, and twenty years later, it is now Ketu Mala's home.

"Before, I was a little girl afraid, asking why do girls not deserve to enter? I was always asking people, but they did not respond, they just said it is tradition. But then my teacher told me, in Buddha's time there were no signposts like this not allowing women into the temple," she says, recalling the moment that she realized it didn't have to be like this.

And not being allowed to do something hasn't stopped Ketu Mala since. There are now thousands of Dhamma Schools in Myanmar, the institutions set up by her foundation, and her religious lectures where she explores how to bring Buddhist principles into your daily life are attended by thousands.

It was at a lecture of this type earlier this year that there was an incident which made her briefly infamous. Although it's hard to imagine this soft-spoken woman clashing with anyone, the Burmese press have it that she "clashed" with a monk in the audience. And not just any monk — a member of the ultra-nationalist, anti-Muslim monastic group that is known in Myanmar as Ma Ba Tha.

"I think he was not happy that for the first time, there is a nun on the stage and he is down on the audience. Myanmar is a male-dominated country, and the monks are always in a higher place, so that's why he was not happy with me and wanted to personally attack me," shrugs Ketu Mala, who says she was "very far" from shouting in response to his aggressive comments.

Ma Ba Tha is not an organization known for its tolerance, particularly of those from other religions — notably, Muslims — and the monk in the audience suggested that the Buddhist concept of *metta*, or loving kindness, should not be handed out to all.

"This is wrong. As a Buddhist monk, he should not say this. Buddha would never talk like this — he says you must have compassion for all people," adds Ketu Mala, giving me the feeling that she was a pretty formidable opponent for the monk, softly spoken or not.

After the incident, some senior monks rallied around to support her, and some MPs, but she also faced a wave of hate speech on Facebook, with Ma Ba Tha followers attacking her. The fact that she shared the stage with a Muslim during the same talk only made matters worse for her opponents.

"There is no need to respond to this," says Ketu Mala curtly, who believes all people and all religions deserve her *metta*, and her help, equally.

Statements like this make me think Ketu Mala truly deserves the word used for nuns in Myanmar (because they cannot be called Bhikkhuni) — *thilashin*. It means owners or protectors of virtue, or ethics. But despite the honorific title, and acts like Ketu Mala's, the *thilashin* are still not taken seriously.

"Even though they are called *thilashin*, they do not have a good impression in society. Many think girls become nuns because they have a problem — no money or no family," says Ketu Mala. "So we have to show that we are coming back and standing up for ourselves. If society accepts that we can, we can do most things."

But Ketu Mala admits it is an uphill battle.

"I think society has forgotten the nuns," she says. "People in Myanmar are more interested now in women's rights and women's empowerment. But the nuns are also women: they are struggling, they face difficulties, they are discriminated against in the religious sector. So I would like our women to remember the nuns."

But remembering and valuing nuns is something Ketu Mala has had problems with even in her own family.

She grew up in Mudon, near Mawlamyine, and her family were, as she describes it, "just the traditional Buddhist", rather than particularly religious. Her decision to drop out of university and become a nun aged just eighteen did not go down well.

"My family did not accept it, so for the first two years it was very hard for me because they cut me off," she says. "I was alone always."

For a young Burmese woman, this would have been even more miserable than it sounds, because it is so unusual. In Burmese culture, it is very rare for women — or indeed, anyone — to be left alone for long periods of time. Families live closely together, cooking together, eating together, sleeping together. So the isolation Ketu Mala must have felt must have been acute.

Despite this, she still believes her decision to become a nun was the best of her life.

"The most important rejection was I had not finished my education. But I chose this way because I wanted to do more Buddhist study. And one thing I always feel is that tomorrow is not sure. So what I want to do, I have to do today," she says.

But it was hard. Her mother did not relent for three or four years, and her relatives and friends kept away too. She has an older brother and sister, and a younger sister as well, all of whom shunned her. It took her father twelve years before he accepted her decision. She is now thirty-six, so the pair have only been reconciled for six years.

"My father thinks I have more capabilities than the other kids so he had big hopes for me, big dreams. There was a documentary made about me recently and in it my father is still sad. He is saying he is proud of me and congratulations, but inside he is still sad — he cried. So other people watching on the television, they tell me they cried as well," she says.

When Ketu Mala went back to university to study in Colombo, Sri Lanka, her father was reassured when she gained a degree. She's now doing a PhD, focusing on the role of nuns in Myanmar, but she thinks her priorities will never match those of her family.

"I am not interested in business, and my family are interested in business. I am interested in how to have a meaningful life, how to spend my power, my strength," she says.

"Burmese lay people sometimes think that nuns live homeless lives, not a successful life. My father, he thinks our little life is not the successful life. I ask him, how do you measure this? They think a valuable life means you have more money or more degrees or more houses. But for me money is not valuable. For me, value is something I can check inside, and what I can do for society."

I ask her how she copes with the isolation she has experienced; not just from her family, but also from religious leaders, the monkhood, who see nuns as separate to them, and from lay people, who also see Ketu Mala and her sisters as being apart from them.

"Since a young age, I have felt strong. Even as a kid I was not afraid. Not like some kids, who are afraid. I have always tried to be a brave kid, a brave girl," says Ketu Mala.

I think it's bravery that is leading her to pursue her goals now, a kind of quiet bravery and dignity that you can see shining in her eyes, behind her rim-less glasses, as she draws herself up to talk about her struggles, from dealing with the family fallout to setting up capacity-building training for nuns, where she "gives them strength and opens their eyes".

But there's something else as well, something we've already touched on in this chapter, which Ketu Mala believes is not only central to Buddhism but also central to life. It's the concept of *metta*, and expanding this concept out into day-to-day life.

That's what her lectures to lay people are about, as well as her regular articles for national newspapers, and even her Facebook posts (she's not only the first feminist nun — she might be the first Facebook nun). It's also how she believes Buddhist principles can help the world to heal. In a country like Myanmar where ethnic conflicts are still raging and peace feels a long way off, Ketu Mala's message has a lot of power. If people listen, that is; remember her lowly position in the eyes of the Burmese public.

Metta is best explained in English as "loving kindness with wisdom", Ketu Mala explains, and her project is called "Loving Kindness and Citizenship".

"Conflicts are largely based on a lack of compassion, and the fear of not understanding each other," she says. "When I talk about kindness and compassion, I do not mean the empty, blind, ill-informed kind. I mean kindness based on knowledge and wisdom. If you look at conflict, it is always based on blind passion with less understanding and sense. My talks always revolve around this."

She extends loving kindness to all of humanity.

"Even if we see bad people, it's our responsibility to straighten them out with the help of sympathy," she says.

Of course, I knew when I interviewed a nun that we would be talking about religion as well as gender, but it's an interesting thing for me, as someone who is not religious, to talk to someone about their religion and to identify with them, and think they are making sense.

"These days, religion has been used up," says Ketu Mala, when I try to explain this. "People hurt each other, using religion as a justification. This is why it's important for us to show where we stand, and there is a certain strength in sharing these beliefs with the public, as a nun."

But perhaps because of her experiences at the hands of organized religion, she is suspicious of it.

"I don't see Buddhism as an institutionalized religion, and I don't conceive myself as a religious leader. I accept myself as a disciple of the Lord Buddha," she says. "The problems I see in the religious sector nowadays is that people fancy themselves as the 'religious leader'. By seeing themselves like this, they start to assert their own selfish ideas, instead of the actual ideas."

"All I ever wanted to be was a disciple, who follows the doctrines and philosophy of the Lord Buddha. Even when I give speeches and sermons, I always tell people to follow the philosophies of Buddha, and it will be ok."

It's a simple message, and listening to it, you can forget that to even be a nun and to dare to give out messages like this, to preach, is something of a revolutionary act.

"The monks can preach the Dharma (Buddha's teaching) on the stage, on thrones, and the nuns are not allowed to preach from here," says

Ketu Mala. "So some people tell me, 'Oh, you are a nun, you do nothing in Buddhism. You have no role, no responsibilities. You do nothing for society.' They say this to me. We are not respected. But I always respond — we have no chance to do anything. The monks have a chance."

A lot of community work is also led by monks, and it is hard for nuns to break in.

"People do not see nuns helping the people, so people have no impression of them. Nuns are not seen as valuable in life," she adds.

In fact, until Ketu Mala, no nuns in Myanmar had ever founded a social work foundation like the Dhamma School Foundation.

"People said no, the nuns won't follow me because I am a nun, because of *phone*," she says. My translator Htun Lynn Zaw breaks in at this point to explain *phone* — it's an idea of male power, which can be lessened by women being either literally or figuratively higher than men.

"This is not a Buddhist idea!" interjects Ketu Mala fiercely. "It is a male-dominated Myanmar idea. It is why women are not allowed in pagodas, near some lakes. They are not auspicious."

Regardless of its origins, this concept is responsible for the traditional distaste for having women (or nuns) at the head of organizations in Myanmar — but also for the old-fashioned superstition that women's *longyi* (the traditional sarong-like garment for both sexes) have to be hung lower than men's, so the men don't lose their *phone*.

Ketu Mala wouldn't say it, because she still has to work with the monks who have decreed that there can be no Bhikkhuni in Myanmar, but I think it's a concept that also has a lot to do with why nuns are banned in the first place: a fear of what they could achieve if a traditionally male sphere of power was properly opened up to them.

With clothing on my mind, I ask Myanmar's feminist nun one more question. Why are her robes brown, when most "renunciants" wear the pink and orange hues that have become so familiar to me from the streets of Yangon?

It's to do with the monastery where she lives, a place where nuns and monks can go everywhere freely, and where their robes match — a sort of equality that isn't even remarked upon, the sort of equality that I think Ketu Mala would like to see in both her religion and her country.

"We are a forest meditation centre, and my teacher, he likes to stay in the forest," she explains gently.

"So as his disciples, nuns and monks, we are forest monks, and we wear the colour of bark. We dye the robes in our monastery, in the colour of the fruit and the sun on the tree."

CHAPTER THREE

The Survivor: Mi Mi

Mᵢ Mᵢ was riding her bike home from work with her father in Thanbyuzyat, Mon state, when it happened.

It was dark.

"When I turned around, I saw his face," she says. "I was talking to my dad while we rode home on our bikes. I knew there was a bike behind us, but I hadn't turned around yet to see who it was. I thought it was just people on their way home like us.

"Then there was a splash. The first splash was on my chest. I turned around to see what it was. Then I saw his face. He splashed the second time right to my face."

The liquid that was splashing was acid, and the "he" splashing it was Mi Mi's ex-boyfriend.

"I cannot find the words to describe the pain," says Mi Mi.

I meet Mi Mi (she does not want to give her real name) in September 2016, six months after the attack, and her injuries are still horrific.

Seriously scarred down one side of her face, she has lost one eye and nearly her ear as well, and her arms and chest are also badly damaged. The injuries are blue and purple and vivid. Her father was also hit during the attack, on his back.

Mi Mi and I meet in a Mon monastery in the centre of Yangon. She stays here when she comes into the country's biggest city for treatment, around once a month.

It's a warm day at the end of rainy season, but it's not too hot, and as we enter the red and gold monastery, my translator and I pass men outside playing *chinlone*, a kind of keepy-uppy/volleyball with a straw ball that is extremely popular in Myanmar. We're welcomed in by a friendly older lady and taken behind a curtained-off section of the monastery. We later find out this is because Mi Mi does not want to go outside, at least not while there are people there.

She smiles as we come in, but her voice breaks when she talks to us. She is only twenty-three years old.

"There is no happiness anymore in my home," she says, when I ask how things are going.

"I don't talk much anymore. I stay in my room, I look at my phone, or I just think. I don't want people to see my face, so I stay in my bedroom. Sometimes my mum stares at me, and I pretend like I don't see, but she is so sad. I know she is."

But while Mi Mi is scarred, both physically and psychologically, she is not scared. In fact, she is spending her time trying to get justice against her attacker — the first women in Myanmar ever to do so for an attack of this type.

"This is happening a lot, but the victims do not really dare to make a case out of it. They just stay in their houses," says Mi Mi, aware that every time she does not do that herself, it requires a major personal struggle.

"One women's organization a few days ago told me that there was a similar case recently in my area, but no one has heard about it because the woman is hiding. But now, if I speak out, there are women out there who will stand up for me and raise awareness. I think if the judges hear about these tragedies, they will start to take these kinds of cases seriously."

There are no statistics about the prevalence of acid attacks in Myanmar, a result of the "culture of silence" that often surrounds violence against women in the country, but women's rights organizations tell me anecdotally that they have seen a marked uptick in recent years.

As such, they say, Mi Mi's case is incredibly important. But sadly, there are major obstacles in her way. Speaking out at all about an attack of this type is both brave and uncommon — as the activist Cheery Zahau explained earlier in this book, domestic violence and rape in Myanmar are seen as issues that are best kept within the family. Police complaints are rare, and investigations and convictions even rarer; in part due to fears of corruption, in part due to the ongoing feeling in some areas of Burmese society that a woman is a man's property, to do with what he will.

Moreover, Myanmar still does not have a proper law regarding violence against women. It relies on the outdated British penal code, and includes no provisions for marital rape, no scope for restraining orders against violent men, and no protection against violence in the home.

While there are robust laws in place punishing rape and sexual abuse, and other forms of assault, corruption in the judiciary and prejudice against women who speak out — plus the lack of hope that the laws they choose will actually help them — often discourage victims from coming forward.

Since 2014, women's organizations have been working with the Ministry of Social Welfare, Relief and Resettlement on the first National Prevention of Violence Against Women Bill. But now it's 2018, and the law has not yet been enshrined.

In the meantime, it's up to brave outliers like Mi Mi to try and push their cases through the courts using the existing legislation, and to face down the prejudice they experience on the way.

On the other hand, in a changing country, Mi Mi does have some support. Her key champions are a pioneering local women's group called Akhaya Women, based in Yangon. From setting up sexual education classes and domestic violence helplines, to launching a campaign encouraging women to whistle for help if they are groped on public transport, they have championed women's rights in Myanmar since 2008, and are now working with Mi Mi.

Founder Htar Htar says the lack of a law to protect women is a travesty. Last year, she told a local news organization: "Domestic violence exists everywhere, and is part of normal life in Myanmar; we don't discuss rape, and we don't report it."

But her organization is committed to changing this, through landmark cases like Mi Mi's, as well as other awareness-raising campaigns.

The legal process, though, won't come cheap, and neither will Mi Mi's extensive and essential treatment. Mi Mi's parents are rubber farmers, and before the attack, Mi Mi had a job as well. She was also about to graduate from university. But now neither she nor her father can work because of their injuries.

Just the first stage of treatment for Mi Mi will cost almost US$15,000 — she'll have to go to Bangkok to find the medical expertise necessary — although the hospital might give her a discount. The legal costs are expected to add at least another US$4,000.

To put that into context, the average income in Myanmar in 2014 was US$1,280 a year, and that takes into account those in urban centres. Rubber farmers in the country's south, like Mi Mi's family, earn far less, making the amounts demanded by Mi Mi's treatment completely out of reach.

In the face of these figures, Akhaya took up the mantle, appealing via Facebook and on the phone, in person and in events across the country, asking ordinary women and men to donate what they can.

That may seem like a big ask in such a poor country, but while Myanmar is poor, it is also almost uniquely generous.

The country's poverty stems back to years of isolation and mismanagement of the economy under the military regime, leaving many of its inhabitants struggling for survival despite the country's natural resources and strategic position between China and India.

Things have improved since 2011, when the military handed over to a military-backed government, and the country's economy began to open up to the world.

However, while the average Burmese person is still a long way from prosperous by global standards, survey after survey has shown that they may be among the world's most generous.

Most recently, the 2016 Charities Aid Foundation World Giving Index found that 91 per cent of Myanmar residents had given money to charity in the last year, 62 per cent said they had helped a stranger, and 55 per cent said they had done some volunteering.

In part, this comes from Buddhism, which encourages the faithful to help others and give to charitable causes. But it also comes from the Burmese tradition of altruism and kindness to your fellow man.

As such, it is unsurprising — but no less inspiring — to hear from Akhaya that they quickly collected 2.2 million kyats (around US$1,600) from Burmese civilians to help with Mi Mi's medical costs.

Other organizations have since stepped in, and Akhaya plans to pay her entire legal bill. After a major Burmese bank contributed a hefty sum, and British readers who saw a story I wrote for a U.K. website about her plight also reached for their wallets, Mi Mi is now nearing at least her initial financial target.

She can't believe so many people are helping her.

"I just want to say thank you. It's hard to find the words to say thank you to these people. It is so helpful, because otherwise I couldn't get any money, any justice, or any treatment," she says.

But the treatment will be an arduous process too. Six months in, it hasn't even properly begun yet. Mi Mi has had three surgeries, but reconstruction is a long way in the future.

"The doctor says he will need a lot of time to do surgery, so I need to be strong — he tells me I need to be fat!" she says, laughing a little.

At the moment, Mi Mi comes to Yangon for injections to soften up the scar tissue and scars ahead of any future operations. Before the injections began, she couldn't even move her head because of how badly damaged the skin was. A tube in her ear stops the ear from closing up completely.

At one point, she apologizes for her pronunciation (she studied English at university, and we speak in a mixture of English and Burmese, via a translator). It's pretty heartbreaking.

"It's not very comfortable for me to move my mouth [in the ways that English pronunciation demands]," she says. "It's hurting now."

The treatment is likely to last for at least five years. This really galls Mi Mi, because even if she does successfully see her attacker imprisoned, he may be released before that.

"If he only goes in there for five years, I will still be doing my treatment, and he will be out and about. It's not fair. I want him to spend as much time in jail as he deserves. It must be justice," she says.

Sadly, as we've seen, getting him in jail in the first place is likely to be as difficult as process — maybe even more so — than the treatment for Mi Mi's suffering skin. The law is not on her side, and unbelievably, but perhaps predictably, neither are many locals.

"He told his parents he didn't do it, and so his brothers, they are angry with me. I should be angry with him, right? But they are angry with me. And some people in the village are saying that it is not true, that another boy did this to me," she says.

But she has no doubt about who attacked her.

"I saw his face, and so did my dad. And I can remember everything. Even in the hospital, I could talk, and my mum asked me who did this, and I told her.

"Then I unlocked my phone, and he called me many times just before the attack," says Mi Mi.

After the attack, the police went to talk to her ex, but he was not at home. They told the local village administrator he was a wanted man, so the official eventually delivered her ex to the police station, but defended him long and loud.

It's a typical story in cases like this. Considering the lack of an official law, the first step by the authorities is often to ask the community elders to investigate or try to sort out the matter, which — as in Mi Mi's case — often isn't at all helpful considering the allegiances and pressures that can be brought to bear upon everyone involved when things are quietly investigated by peers. In fact, a 2014 survey by Action Aid suggested the "sort it out amongst yourselves" tactic had led to a "culture of impunity" for domestic attacks in Myanmar.

Despite the best efforts of the village administrator, though, the boy who attacked Mi Mi is currently in jail until a court date is set.

His behaviour fit into an abusive pattern, Mi Mi admits. The pair had been friends for about seven months before they got together. They dated for six months, and he attacked her three months to the day after she broke up with him.

The pair split up because of his jealousy and anger issues, and things only got worse after the break-up.

"He was giving me threatening calls, but I didn't really tell my family. I thought it was our own mess to clean up," says Mi Mi.

"He was saying hurtful things about me, but I did not retaliate. He once said: 'I will make your life a living hell, I will make you feel dead while you are alive.' He also threatened my family, my parents who go out into the dark at night. He was monitoring me and my family. I knew something would happen one day or another."

Mi Mi has already faced her attacker in preliminary court hearings, although he has yet to officially appear. In fact, he snuck into the court to gawp at her while she gave her evidence.

"The court did not tell me that he was behind me, because they thought I might be scared of him," she says.

"The judge immediately ordered him to leave, but I intentionally turned around to stare at him. He did not look back at me, of course. I am not scared of him. At all."

From what she remembers, it doesn't appear that he showed much remorse.

"He was smiling and pulling faces like nobody could hurt him. He was acting. My mum was so angry with him when she saw his face," says Mi Mi.

But for all her bravado — "I'm not afraid, because [what he had done], it's already the worst thing he could do" — Mi Mi found appearing in court in front of so many people a harrowing experience.

"I didn't want to go," she admits. "There were so many people looking at me, all just staring. I felt like I had no power to stand in front of them. I wanted to disappear."

But Mi Mi has an inner core of steel. I ask her if she thinks she is brave enough to go through the whole case.

"I think I am brave enough," she says, which is brave in itself.

"Some people have said to me, it's ok, you don't have to do this — but even when he threw acid at me, I didn't cry. I didn't shout. I just stayed quiet."

She isn't staying quiet anymore, regardless of what it costs her personally.

"The acid attack was unbearable. I never wanted to feel this way, and this attack will be with me for life. If he goes to jail for a long period of time, it will scare off other potential attackers," she says.

Thinking about the future is still hard for Mi Mi; the years of treatment ahead of her stalk her thoughts, and stifle her dreams.

"I get depressed, but then I think in another way I should be strong, because I have a lot to do," she says. "Like my mum says, I'm still young. People are doing their best for me, and that gives me the power to be brave and not fear anything."

She says she doesn't hate men, and one day thinks she might have another boyfriend.

"Every man is not like this," she says. "Maybe one day."

Before the attack, she wanted to go to Yangon or even abroad to study accountancy or work, after finishing her English degree. She used to fight about it with her parents.

"My mum told me, no, you have to stay here with me. 'In the morning you go to work then in the evening you come back to me, that's enough,' she said. So then we argued, but now she is feeling so sad, because she says she didn't let me go anywhere, and made me stay home. And now, she says, because of her, I really can't go anywhere, and I have to stay at home."

And while Mi Mi's dreams to go abroad and work have taken a hit, that's what she is still aiming for when her treatment ends in five years.

"Maybe in five years' time, I can work, I can go out with people," she says. "I think at that time I will be better than now, if I can have surgery for my neck and eyes, I'll be able to work. That's my hope."

Since the attack though, she is now considering working to help other women as well as in the accountancy role she had initially planned for.

"I want life for women in future to be better than my life. Maybe I will work for the women. I see a lot of women attacked in Myanmar," she says.

She laughs wryly when I ask her if I think life generally is hard for women in Myanmar, then starts to speak in low, passionate Burmese.

"That is so true. Especially in rural areas, people tell girls don't do this or don't do that. Girls spend their lives housekeeping or in the kitchen, and even if they go out to work, housekeeping is still their duty.

"Then there are a lot of cases I hear about — husbands coming home drunk and hitting their wives violently. It's very unfair for the girls," she says.

And she believes the only way to change things is if women are allowed to legislate for their own futures — perhaps even women like her.

"Since the laws were written by men, how could they possibly know how women feel? Laws for women should be written by women themselves," she says.

But for now, she has a smaller, sadder hope. It's just to graduate.

She finished her English degree before the attack, and her plan was to go to the graduation ceremony in Yangon this year with some friends to collect her qualification. But now she is not sure she can face it.

"My dream is that I want to go and get my degree, and attend the celebration. But I cannot dream that," she says, then pauses, before looking down and speaking more quietly.

"I don't have the self-confidence to go out in front of all those people," she says. "I always have to cover my face when I go out with my hair, or with glasses, and with long sleeves, or people are looking at me, and staring at me, and I just ... I can't afford that."

It's a sad reminder that, despite all of Mi Mi's strength — and she is strong — she still doesn't feel strong enough for this one small act; robbed of something she deserves by a man who still may never face what he deserves.

CHAPTER FOUR

The Businesswoman: Yin Myo Su

YIN MYO SU is probably Myanmar's most famous cat-lover.
This makes it a little disconcerting when she tells me, moments after we meet for the first time at her floating hotel on Inle Lake, that she doesn't like cats.

"You will laugh, but I hate cats," she says, looking down at the blue-grey felines slinking affectionately around her legs. "When I was little, kittens near my house would come and hurt my puppy's nose."

The cats blink their golden eyes and look back up at her. "I do not like cats," she repeats, firmly.

But love them or hate them, she has become known for them — not just in Myanmar, but across the world. Yin Myo Su, a hotelier by trade, found out in 2007 that the world-renowned Burmese cat barely existed at all in its homeland, Burma. So she began a mission to bring them back.

Working with a couple of heritage organizations, and starting off with just seven cats bought from collectors around the world at eye-watering expense — including breeders in Australia and the pet department of London's Harrods department store — she now has around forty felines, living on an island of their own (I'm not joking) on the picturesque lake in Shan State, attached to the hotel she runs. She lives at another hotel, across the lake.

The cats are housed in mini-replicas of Burmese royal palaces, a nod to their rumoured heritage as palace guards for Burma's ancient kings and queens. Their home is called the Burmese Cat Village, and signposted as such. They have pedicures and manicures, family planning, a dedicated staff, and even a honeymoon suite. One of them even tweets (@Phyuley).

Some are given away to locals, and foreigners can also buy the beasts, at a price-tag of US$600. Aung San Suu Kyi even had one, but she had to give it back because her dog was jealous.

The project is about more than just pet cats, though.

"I see Burma losing the things we have, like jade, and as the country opens up we could do something that would preserve our heritage," says Yin Myo Su, a petite, forty-four-year-old bustling businesswoman, who usually dresses in jewelled colours and is known to most as Misuu.

"People say to me 'Why cats?', but why not?"

She hopes the cat project can teach Burmese people that their heritage is something to be valued, even if remembering the recent past can sometimes be painful. And the cats themselves have changed her opinions — she now has two of her own, and says they taught her about independence and how to love.

"It's important to go back to your roots," she adds. "A tree that has very strong, deep roots is unlikely to fall."

Misuu herself has strong, deep roots: far from being just a mad cat lady (an English term she learned and hates, having been labelled as one in newspaper articles), she's also an incredibly successful businesswoman and a passionate advocate for her native Shan State.

Haunted by the voice of her sixteen-year-old self, who left Myanmar after getting into trouble for political activism in 1988, she has barely paused for breath since, opening several hotels, an eco-project, and a small vocational training school. She has become an inspirational figure for women in a country where success in the business world is rare if you wear a *htamein* rather than a *longyi* (respectively, female and male traditional dress in Myanmar).

It has kept her busy. "I will stop working when I die," she laughs.

Two birthdays frame Misuu's story. First, her nineteenth, in Thailand, which she spent on the streets.

"On my nineteenth birthday, I had no money, and no food," she says, laughing a little at how ridiculous it sounds. But she quickly corrects herself: "No, I can't laugh. It was not funny at the time. I had no idea how I would end up."

To work out how she got there we have to go a couple of years further back, to 1988. It was a pivotal moment for so many of the women in this book and indeed for all Burmese people — and it was a dark one in Burmese history.

While there had been several uprisings in Myanmar since General Ne Win's seizure of power in 1962, which marked the opening of the era of military rule and the ensuing spiralling of the once-proud nation into a place of poverty, brutality and fear, none had had quite the impact of the mass 1988 protests.

Led by students and other young people who became known as the 88 generation, protests began on 8 August 1988, giving the pro-democracy uprising its name — 8888. Hundreds of thousands of students, monks, doctors, children and housewives took to the streets after the initial protests spread, first in Yangon, then across the country. Aung San Suu Kyi, daughter of independence hero General Aung San, became the face of a nation's hopes for democracy when she appeared near Shwedagon Pagoda and called for a peaceful resolution to the stand-off.

It was not to be. Instead, a different faction of the army took power in a bloody military coup (the State Law and Order Restoration Council) on 18 September. Throughout the protests, unarmed demonstrators had been beaten, sometimes to death, imprisoned, shot and raped. The generals orded the army to shoot to kill, and in the final brutal put-down, the military showed no mercy. Thousands were killed, and others were chased into the jungle.

Aung San Suu Kyi pleaded with the world: "I would like every country in the world to recognize the fact that the people of Burma are being shot down for no reason at all." But it was to no avail. The uprising was over.

For Misuu, a sixteen-year-old girl in Shan state, it was a scary time.

"I was on the street as a sixteen-year-old, I gave speeches, I was a very angry complaining teenager. All teenagers complain, but for me I was lucky — well, not lucky for my country, but lucky that my negative energy that I wanted to give to my family, my school — I could give that to '88," she remembers.

"So my energy was put in the right direction, but then you point fingers, and it gets back to you," she says.

Many of her friends from that time were killed or escaped to exile.

"So you say, ok, my life, I have to dedicate for my friends who died on the street, in the jungle, in the prison. I have to live the life they cannot live anymore, because they have died already," says Misuu.

"I don't want that loss — instead I want to live for the many, many people who did not get the chance to continue."

Two years later, her father — who had been running a guest house on Inle Lake since 1976 with Misuu's mother, and shared Misuu's politics — bravely stood for election in the 1990 elections as a candidate for Aung San Suu Kyi's new political party, the National League for Democracy (NLD).

The elections were a disaster: despite the NLD winning 80 per cent of the seats, the military junta dismissed the results and proceeded to put many of the party's candidates in prison, including Misuu's father, U Ohn Maung.

Just before his arrest, Misuu's mother sensed the way things were going, and sent her fiery, political daughter away. At first, she went to Switzerland, to a hotel school there, to learn the family business.

"When I was away, my father was arrested. He didn't want me to know. So then some of my friends said to me I'm so sorry for your dad, and I knew something had happened. So I came home," says Misuu.

But her mother was still protecting her as well as she could. She kicked Misuu out of the house to try to get her out of danger. It was a very real danger: see Wai Wai Nu's chapter (Chapter 8) for what happened to the children of activists who stuck around.

"So first I went to Switzerland, but then guess what? My father was in prison. I was broke. My mum kicked me out and I ended up in Thailand, practically on the street," says Misuu.

Misuu, who knows she comes from a privileged background by Burmese standards, says the experience of being so alone and hungry for those few years, including on her nineteenth birthday, taught her some serious lessons.

"That was a period I starved and felt quite insecure, and I learned the food is front of you is very precious. You should not waste any food, because you will be starving at one time in your life. I learnt my lesson," she says.

"So you think I should complain, oh it was so horrible being starved? No. It allowed me to understand the value of food and it made me a more flexible person."

She was saved by her father's tourism contacts, and her own initiative. As the only guest house at Inle Lake in the previous few decades, her family had welcomed guests from Europe for years. Some had become friends.

"So I got connected with them again and told them, 'Here I am on the street. Shall I go home and be put in jail, or will you help me?'" says Misuu. "That was it: they sent me a flight ticket and I ended up in France by accident."

It changed her life.

She learned French fast because she concentrated on the language rather than worrying about her father imprisoned in the notorious Insein Jail. He was released in 1992.

"My dad being in prison, that was bad, but it drove me to make a difference, to bring back my knowledge and spread it," says Misuu. "And where do you think I would be without all this hardship? Thank god I had challenges. Without this I wouldn't be focused, I would be a spoiled woman who has everything but doesn't know how to make the most out of it."

While she was in France, Misuu also fell in love with museums (she fell in love with a Frenchman too, who later became her husband and the father of her children, but more about him later).

"France is my adopted country, which really made me understand about conservation and preservation. In Europe, you guys are so good at preserving your heritage," she says.

"Museums, like literature, music, this is something that nourishes your heart and soul, and humans need it. It's inspiration, and respect for the generation before, sharing it with the coming generation. So when

I visited the national museum in Yangon a couple of years ago, I cried, literally, because the beautiful things we have are not presented properly here, and we have many more collections we could have but we have not put enough effort into them."

Her love for museums was the first spark for her ultimate business philosophy, shown in the cat project at Inle, that preserving heritage and maintaining a successful private business can and indeed should be intertwined.

That's why Misuu's roster of business interests — as well as her family's clutch of hotels, of which more later — now includes the hotel for cats and guests, who are housed in traditional floating bungalows and fed Misuu's grandmother's recipes; the small vocational training centre on-site, which teaches the next generation of hoteliers for next-to-no-fees; and an aquarium and testing facilities to support the environmental protection of the lake, which has seen dramatic falls in water quality as tourism in the area has taken off in recent years.

"Inle Heritage was my window, and it's the only project I've ever done totally alone. It reflects my forty-four years of life, taking revenge for those struggling moments and turning it into this," she says. All of the businesses reflect Misuu's philosophy: using, preserving and celebrating the past to succeed in the present and provide a launch pad for the future.

The vocational training school project was supported by a loan from a Norwegian NGO, which Misuu is now paying back. The other 50 per cent of the start-up costs were covered by Misuu's own money. The other projects are self-financing, and indeed some make a profit, something Misuu is proud of, arguing that no entrepreneur can sacrifice running a successful business at the altar of heritage. The entire enterprise is now close to completely covering its own costs — NGO/charity elements and all — a rare thing in this field.

Now she is building a bamboo school for local kids, and wants to set up franchises.

"I want to go into franchising, marketing for young entrepreneurs who want to run their own businesses to make sure people can shape their lives in the way they want using their own hands," she says.

"There's a Burmese saying about a big tree hosting 10,000 birds. My idea is that it's better to create a forest with many, many trees, with their own sky, their own rain, their own birds. If something like Cyclone Nargis hits again, one big tree standing alone will fall down and the birds, I don't know where they will go, but if we have a forest, maybe some will fall but some are still there to help each other. Together we are stronger."

It's a particularly persuasive and philanthropic philosophy in a country which is just getting to grips with the demands of international business, something Misuu and her family have worked in for decades. She is a realist, and understands that getting Myanmar on its feet again will cost money — and ideally, she believes that money can come from within, from Burmese entrepreneurs.

As she said in a talk she once gave, she has always been a troublemaker, and now she is asking troublesome questions of business. Firstly, if I can run a business that does all this, that makes money and does the right thing, why can't others? And secondly, if I, as a woman in a developing country cut off from the world and without many resources can make it work, why can't a big corporation?

But before Misuu reached a point where she could ask these questions, there were many obstacles in her business life for her to overcome.

On her return to Myanmar in the 1990s, Misuu first started working at her family's hotel, the small guest house on Inle Lake. At the same time, her family set up another hotel in Pindaya, also in Shan State. She also worked with her father and a group from the Pa'O tribe, another Shan State ethnic group, to set up the Golden Island Cottages on their land after a ceasefire with the government. The jewel in the family's crown, the Inle Princess — still run by Misuu, and easily the best hotel on the lake — was also established over the next few years. The family now also own a hotel in Mrauk-U, Rakhine State.

All was going well. Although Misuu's dad had been banned from politics for ten years, he could work in the hotel industry, and the family felt relatively safe. Safe enough, in fact, that they even dared to put mini-coded protests into the hotels themselves — the lampshades looked like the hat symbol of the NLD, and the uniforms were NLD colours.

In 2006, Misuu took on a job managing two properties in Inle and Bagan with her team.

"But political instability, I didn't count on it. Natural disaster, I forgot about it. And guess what? I took over these two properties, invested so much money, energy, and time — and on paper, the vision is super cool," she says.

"But then the Saffron Revolution [another uprising, also suppressed, this time led by monks] came, and we started losing everything. Then Cyclone Nargis [a huge storm, Myanmar's worst ever natural disaster, which killed around 138,000 people and caused catastrophic destruction]. Our expectation had been 70 per cent occupancy, and we ended up with not even 20," says Misuu.

She took her staff — almost 600 people — to one side and explained the business was close to bankrupt.

"But what saved me was the team," she says. "Some proposed time off with half pay, some volunteered to leave the jobs for those who really needed them, and others said they would leave and find jobs in hospitality in Dubai and Qatar. So I recommended them to the hotels and they said if I needed them back some day, I could count on them. Which was true! They came back. So when you are in a community you are never alone."

Doing business under the junta, when corruption was out of control, was another challenge.

"Sometimes people say ... is a 'white' tycoon, a 'black' tycoon, or blacklisted — honestly, all of us here who survived during those difficult years are grey," she says.

"My family never killed anyone for our business, we never imported arms, or drugs, or stole or used dirty money or did money laundering. But the system was so corrupt."

She remembers trying to pay tax aged twenty-four – despite the fact that she had no idea what her taxes went to pay for, considering that her family built everything from scratch for their hotels, from an electricity system to a well for water for the properties.

The local tax officer took her aside, explaining that if she paid, the bill would only go up the next year, and any problems paying would be taken very seriously.

"Then he said, 'No one else wants to pay. You can afford it but the roadside restaurant cannot. You're making their lives miserable,'" she recalls.

Finally, he explained his own situation. "'Do you know how many children I have? Do you know what school they are at? Do you know how much that costs, and do you know how much my salary is?' he asked. He made less than US$150 a month, and the fees were US$300," says Misuu.

"'You know where I get that money? If you don't support me, you think my family can survive? Sorry, that's the truth. I'm ashamed, you are willing to do the right thing, but I have to show you the reality.'"

Misuu shrugs.

"Am I corrupt? Did I participate in corruption? Yes, you do. Everyone in this country was conditioned to be corrupt so they could control us, because you are always making one mistake. They make you make one mistake so if they want to grab you, they can grab you. You live in fear. Everyone is grey in this country."

She points out that she now pays 100 per cent tax under the new government.

Then, for a moment, this vibrant, capable woman looks a little tired. Perhaps it's the strain of explaining, over and over, what life was like back then — or perhaps she is just remembering how hard it was to live it.

Despite her insistence that her team and family were with her every step of the way, it is her second story of a birthday, then, that really shows me something about Misuu as a woman — and, when I think about it, about successful women not only in Burma but around the world.

This time, Misuu was turning forty, and was overseas. Her marriage was struggling, her businesses were demanding, and she was working abroad.

"I was away for a month from my team, my family, my kids, and in a country where I knew no one. I really got my time back, and guess what? Everybody forgot my fortieth birthday: my children, my parents, my husband, my brother," says Misuu.

I must look shocked, because she says briskly: "Don't worry, it's just a number." Then she pauses.

"But it made me realize, oh my god, the reason people don't remember is because I organize everything. I do so much people don't know how to do anything anymore. And people depending on you all the time is not healthy."

It was a transformative moment.

"I can't be like a carpet, you know? So I need to work on that, and I did that on my fortieth birthday. That was like my meditation moment, and I came home and was like, I don't want that. I want you to sort yourselves out!"

It's a battle cry that many women might recognize. I think about a friend's mum in the U.K., who buys her own birthday presents because her family wouldn't remember to do so, or the fact that women all over the world are still seen as the primary caregivers for their children despite both partners working full-time.

For Misuu, it was perhaps even more complicated. After a fairy-tale romance — she met her husband in France, and he told her on the night they met that they would marry — he came to work in the family business in Inle.

It led to a decades-long role for Misuu as the facilitator and in-between for a trio of men: her father, her husband (they split up three years ago, although he still lives in Inle. Misuu does not want to talk too much about the breakdown of their relationship), and the business's financial controller, a man so close she calls him uncle.

"I have to recognize I did a good goddamn job," she says. "The three of them are Sunday-born, we call it a *garuda* [a mythical bird, thought to be the scourge of snakes]. And I am Wednesday evening, a Rahu, so I am an elephant without tusks."

She pauses, then says almost to herself: "I don't know why they didn't allow me to have tusks. That would have been much easier."

She continues: "We have a saying that one *garuda* is so strong that it can shake an elephant. And I have three *garuda* on me, one shaking my head, one my body, one my tail. And sometimes they cannot get on at all, these unbearable macho men."

No matter how hard they tried, I doubt that those pesky *garuda* managed to shake Misuu too badly — and the success of the family business speaks to that. But she doesn't blame them for their shaking either, or their macho egos. In fact, Misuu believes that the Burmese attitudes to gender are as much of a prison for men as they are for women.

"The way we raise boys is wrong," she says (she and her ex-husband have a son and a daughter, in their late teens, whom they have tried to raise as equals).

"They have all these pressures that girls do not have — they have different pressures — but when the boys are babies, they are put in this man box and told they have to suffer in silence."

She believes men in Myanmar are in a state of panic, in much the same way as some in the Western world have argued that there is a crisis in masculinity here, too. Traditionally, in Myanmar, women have held power in the home (to an extent), says Misuu. But now that women are also growing more powerful outside the home, Misuu says men have not been equipped to handle it, or to be able to see the two sexes as equal — and to understand their own role in the new world.

"So men feel like you are already powerful at home and you want a job outside, to be equal to me? What is my place then? They got scared. Boys are doubly discriminated — that whole don't cry like a girl, that kind of girl, that's repressing both genders," she says.

While she says being a woman has occasionally been challenging in business, she is adamant that on her team it's harder for the men, who, when faced with problems, can't deal with them emotionally because of how they are raised. Moreover, they can't deal with other people's emotions. But she says men remain more resistant than women to the idea that the changing situation for women can help both genders. For example, she says whenever she tries to talk to men about women's empowerment or feminism, the most common response is "oh god".

"But I want to say to them, you don't need to lead if you don't want to, women can lead. It is freedom now. Taking men out from this box, this is gender equality, this will liberate you.

"My liberation as a woman is related to your liberation as a man. I want men not to freak out about this! Feminists are not always complaining! I want to liberate all of you," she says.

This message is another one of her missions, alongside the importance of remembering Myanmar's heritage as business pours into the country. She touches on these themes throughout her public appearances, both at home and internationally, at leadership events and even when she was asked to give a TEDx talk.

With this to-do list, and considering she also runs several businesses, I'm unsurprised when she tells me she normally wakes up around 6.00 a.m. She used to immediately check her email — although now she tries to do some exercises or yoga first — before heading for breakfast, lunch and dinner meetings with so many different guests that she sometimes only eats a course with each visitor.

Right now, she's busy building her new school, for children in villages near the lake. Like most people who live on the lake — the Inthar — she gets boats from place to place as easily as most people walk, bike or drive.

Misuu tries to make time to see her parents as well, who live nearby, but since the landmark 2015 elections, she sees her dad a little less. Twenty-five years after he was first elected, U Ohn Maung won his seat for the NLD, and is now tourism minister.

Misuu is very proud, but it's another worry. She loves her father, but tries hard to separate him from the minister in her mind. This is partly for conflict of interest purposes, but also for when she disagrees with him.

"This is a unique chance for us to get back to how it was before 1962 (when General Ne Win took over ruling Burma and introduced the disastrous Burmese Way to Socialism). People were coming and saying they want to catch up with Rangoon," says Misuu.

"But the thing with this government, which is composed of people like my father — grey-haired people, generals … I think if they really want to make a difference, they need other people, poor people. But for now I think if they are successful they can be 70 per cent max. There is so much to do."

She feels the country is at a moment when things could go either way, and hopes what does happen can be an example for other emerging democracies and developing economies.

"We want people to look at us and say, oh they had a bad time, but look, they survived. They came on. We can teach the world, we just need to make it right," she says.

She doesn't think this is only the government's job. In fact, she's added it to her own to-do list (and having met her, I think this can only be a good thing for her country — although she says she's not looking for political office herself).

"We can share good practice, share things, teach. It's like my team — if I can keep them focused, they stay focused, and keep others focused, willing to be generous and help others. This is a model we should be replicating. I saw a talk once where a bunch of people from places were saying oh we had a chance [in developing countries], but we screwed most people and we regret it. We had multibillions of dollars but we screwed up a lot of things trying to help, and now we've got to fix it.

"Hearing these people — oh my god — if we could learn from them and make them feel someone listened, and wants to avoid those mistakes, that would be so great."

Such grand aims maybe sound a little over the top for a hotelier, but Misuu isn't satisfied to sit back.

"Of course I complain sometimes, but then I compare my life to the boys selling jasmine flowers between the cars, or cigarette packs on the street. And I'm sitting in an air-conditioned car, you know. I can't complain," she says.

You could argue, though, that she could afford to rest on her laurels a bit, with a string of successful businesses in her wake, a happy family, and fully formed, influential, philosophies on business, gender and preserving the past now permeating through Burmese culture and beyond.

But Misuu says she will always be driven by the voice of her sixteen-year-old self, and the friends she lost.

She says her biggest fear is letting herself down.

"All this goes back to when I was a teenager and pointing fingers," she says.

"Now I am over forty, and I am in a position where I can make a difference, and guess what? That little girl in me, the young troublemaker pointing fingers at everyone ... I am so scared that one day my daughter or other boys and girls of that age will be pointing and saying she couldn't make a difference, you didn't make a difference.

"I don't want to have the finger pointed at me saying you didn't make the right choice. Maybe people think this is amazing but I would say I am haunted by my own voice. If you point the finger at someone, there are always fingers pointing back at you."

And with that, she leaves the café where we are talking, and heads to another meeting.

CHAPTER FIVE

The Environmental Campaigner and Princess: Devi Thant Cin

W HEN I go to meet Devi Thant Cin, I get lost — even though she lives on one of the most famous roads in Yangon, metres away from the Buddhist symbol of a nation, the shining, golden Shwedagon Pagoda, and next to the tomb of the country's last queen.

I call in a panic, and a small, friendly woman appears at a gate close to a small stall selling 3-in-1 coffee sachets. She waves at me from behind a grinning betel nut vendor.

"Come in, come in, here I am," she beams, taking my arm and ushering me in to her two-storey half-wooden, half-concrete house. It's homely, but basic; you go in through a part-glass lean-to, and then snaking wooden stairs lead past boxes of papers and shelves groaning with pictures, rocks, and small statues.

In a way, that's what threw me in the first place. You see, before I met Devi Thant Cin, I already knew she was a princess. She is descended from Myanmar's last royals, King Thibaw and Queen Supalayat, who were deposed and exiled by the British colonialists nearly 150 years ago in 1885.

I'd been told that her family had been given the house by the former British governor of Myanmar (then Burma), Sir Reginald Hugh-Dorman Smith, in the 1940s. Given the general British respect for royalty (once they have stripped them of any actual power, of course, and at the safe distance of a few generations), I'd assumed that the descendants would have been given something a bit more, well, palatial.

Devi thinks this is funny.

"I have lived here for fifty years," she says simply. "It was given to my grandfather for religious purposes, to look after the tomb of Queen Supalayat [the last queen of Burma, and Devi's great-grandmother]."

She shares the house with two other royal descendant families. Her attitude gives me a clue about her general attitude towards her glittering genealogy. It's a fact, and she is proud of it, but she doesn't really expect anything because of it; and in fact, she would be horrified if she was treated differently because of it.

The only real clues that it is a house of royalty lie in a sign on the wall outside, offering English tuition by the King's great-grandnephew, and an ageing oil painting on the walls inside, a snapshot of the royals themselves — Devi's great-grandparents — which she has vowed never to sell despite its likely high price-tag.

Maintaining the painting is expensive too, though, so seventy-year-old Devi uses the traditional method to keep mildew at bay: half a potato run along the surface. You get the impression that for Devi, royalty — even remembered royalty, like her own — is more about duties like this than palaces.

"What I do is as important as who I am," she says. "Yes, yes, yes."

And what she does is why I'm here. Devi is an environmental activist, possibly Myanmar's first, certainly one of its most prominent. And in a country where the focus is on much-needed development of the economy rather than protecting its resources, her work is vital.

Indeed, Devi's royal ancestors would barely recognize their country. According to the UN's Food and Agriculture Organization (FAO), in 2010 Myanmar had the third-highest rate of forest reduction in the world, only outstripped by Brazil and Indonesia. Only about half of the country is still covered in forest after decades of exploitation for logging — an area the size of Brunei is lost every year.

Fish stocks have collapsed due to overfishing, waste management is rarely prioritized, and major schemes — such as dams or oil pipelines — proceed without any thought for the natural resources that lie in their paths. Sewage leaks into pristine seas, mining tears up ancient landscapes, and recognized flora and fauna diversity hotspots, housing animals from tigers to the rare Irrawaddy dolphin, are increasingly under threat.

At the same time, from the military junta onwards, Myanmar's governments have focused on other things — then, power and repression, and now, growth — and have turned their backs on the environment. For example, just 0.2 per cent of the country's national budget goes towards looking after its protected natural areas.

All of the factors above spurred Devi into action back in the early 2000s, when the generals still had the country in their grip. In 2007, she launched her own — Myanmar's first and, still, only — environmental magazine *Aung Pin Lae* becoming one of the few voices in Myanmar to draw any attention to the global green movement.

It was a challenge, and a brave act: the aim was to enlighten the Burmese about the environmental treasures on their doorsteps, and the risks these treasures were facing, at a moment when any dissent was often brutally quashed.

She relied upon help from her friends and fellow activists to get the magazine off the ground — her royal background does not mean a royal allowance — and many thought she was crazy.

"When we first published this," she says, brandishing a copy of the magazine, "Some of my colleagues said, 'Oh Devi, you are mad, no one will read your magazine. Nobody is interested, it's not the right time it's not the right time.' But ... I know the ecosystem is changing globally and in the West they are studying environmental issues, right from primary school.

"But in Myanmar, this word 'environment' is just for intellectuals, people don't care about it. So ... slowly, slowly."

She laughs as she remembers how difficult the early years were, and shrugs off any concerns about her own safety, suggesting the junta had bigger fish to fry.

She started the magazine with just 15 *lakh* (1,500,000 kyat — around US$1,120) from one of her friends and there were many occasions when she struggled to keep the publication afloat.

"It was for sale, you know, in bookshops and things, but I struggled a lot. My friends told me it was nonsense but I told them no, it cannot be. Someday it will be precious for our country, because globally the key issue will be the environment. So we must prepare now," she says.

Things eased a little with backing from the Forest Resource Environment Development and Conservation Association (FREDA; a large NGO in Myanmar) and particularly its then-chairman, U Ohn — now nearly ninety — who won some money from a global environmental award and passed some on to Devi.

"He told me, 'You must carry on,'" says Devi. So she did.

Realizing that there was strength in numbers (even small ones), Devi then gathered together the handful of environmental activists in Burma and formed the Global Green Group (3G), followed closely by the Myanmar Green Network.

It is a kind of environmental advisory board, made up of mining engineers, meteorologists, lawyers, civil engineers, activists, researchers and journalists, who all work together as volunteers.

"Our main aim is to be the check and balance between the government and civil society," says Devi. What this means in practice is standing up for the environment — and the people living within it — when either or both are threatened by rampant development.

Most famously, this has meant leading protests against the Myitsone dam, a controversial project backed by China at the mouth of the Irrawaddy River in Kachin state. Polls suggest that around 85 per cent of Myanmar's residents are against the dam, which would mainly supply energy to China while decimating the local area, which is seen as a special place for many Burmese.

"If there is dam construction that they shouldn't do, we point out that it's not the time to do it," says Devi, simply.

Regarding Myitsone, she adds: "For the whole of Myanmar, the Irrawaddy is like the mother river. And for the Kachin state, this area is heritage for them. We must be careful."

In part thanks to Devi's efforts, the project is currently on hold. A governmental decision is expected in the next few months, although there have been delays as a result of renewed ethnic conflict in the area.

If the project gets the go-ahead, Devi and her colleagues will not take it lying down.

Back in 2013, she told local magazine *The Irrawaddy*: "If anyone tries to resume the project, I will continue to protest." Her position has not changed.

The Green Network team also has the scientific firepower to conduct soil and water tests to work out the potential environmental impact of developments, giving local protests more welly. They did this at the Letpadaung copper mine in northwest Myanmar, another controversial China-backed project. This project is now going ahead, despite ongoing protests.

The team also provide a key, massively neglected function in Myanmar: simply telling the public living near the proposed developments what might happen to their area and the people living within it if the work goes ahead. One of the most shocking things as a journalist when travelling around Myanmar is meeting people living close to huge industrial developments — which at best mean a huge change to their lives and livelihoods, as many are subsistence farmers, and at worst mean forced relocation or the confiscation of their land — is the extent to which they are kept in the dark by the developers and the government.

In extremis, sometimes the citizens don't know anything about what is about to happen to them until their land is taken from them. That was a favoured junta tactic during the military years, but it's by no means a historical one even in modern day Myanmar.

"We give them small documents, the people who would be affected. We ask, 'What's the catch?' So now they know," says Devi. In some situations, the team also brings the developer to meet the local communities affected by their work — to see how the children are finding it harder to breathe, how the fish have died, or how the crops have failed.

"This is the reality, and it can be dangerous. But we want them to see with their own eyes. So we protest," says Devi.

Her latest initiative is all about bamboo, which grows plentifully all around Myanmar. Her aims with the new group, the Bamboo Lovers Network, established in 2014, are manifold. Burmese people work with bamboo a lot — many houses are built from it — but they don't use the crop strategically, Devi says.

"Our people, they just cut it and use it, they do not re-plant. They think there is lots of forest, there's no need to plant again. So we educate them and give knowledge on this," she says.

This education protects the forest but also prevents the people from being exploited.

"We also give knowledge on how there is a big international market for bamboo. The Chinese come and buy our bamboo seed, but our people do not know the seed cannot be planted again. Bamboo is natural for them, not systematically grown from seeds," she explains.

Encouraging bamboo use above plastic not just in Myanmar but globally is also far more sustainable, and is actually a green goal in the international market.

"I give interviews about this to journals, magazines, online, and I visit," says Devi.

"The first time we went to the village, I told them you'd better pick up the bamboo seeds, and people asked me what for. I explained that you can get more trees, but they told me there's lots of forest naturally. So I explain that we must preserve the forests, so we can get the quality materials. Preserve the forests first."

The extent to which Devi's job involves awareness raising and capacity building is one of the ways that the role of an environmentalist differs in Myanmar than in other countries. She is incredibly busy, and resolutely cheerful and determined despite the demands on her: her phone rings almost non-stop while we speak, and she sees her voice as vital in getting the message out.

In fact, in the way that you see royal families around the world gracing hospices, charities and causes with their presence, Devi does the same for the green movement in Myanmar: uncomplainingly taking on this burden, despite the fact that the royal onus on her to do so has largely withered away.

"I have to be an activist because we are all living on this planet," she says simply. "We aren't separate from the environment, if we cut down the trees, drain the oceans, the mountains, the air — it is all connected, because we are living on earth. So if global warming is coming, we will all be impacted."

And while Devi doesn't want to trade on her royal background — sometimes refusing to attend events if the company booking her talk about her ancestry rather than her activism — she's aware that sometimes it can be a draw that is worth capitalizing on if it means more people will listen to what she is saying about the natural world.

"I tell them, but I'm not coming as a princess. I don't want to show off that I am the great-granddaughter. It doesn't matter. I come to give knowledge and inspire and educate for the environment. Do not mention it, or I will not come," she says, defiantly.

But she is beginning to understand that her star power comes, uniquely, both from her green credentials and her golden ones. She's even been dubbed "Myanmar's Green Princess" by one Brit making a film investigating the fate of the lost royal family.

And those golden credentials are as shiny as they come, even if Devi doesn't like to dust them off. Her father, himself known as the "Red Prince" for his Marxist views, was the son of King Thibaw and Queen Supalayat's last child, the fourth princess.

The fourth princess — Devi's grandmother — was born in exile in Ratnagiri, India, after her parents were ousted by an invading British army led by Lord Randolph Churchill (father of Winston) in 1885. It was an abrupt and undignified exit: British forces riding high on conquering much of Burma and absorbing it into their Indian empire were aggrieved by Thibaw's insistence on independence and respect, including his demands that they remove their shoes on royal visits.

The family were kicked out of the palace in Mandalay on a bullock cart, accompanied by their two young daughters, while the queen was pregnant with their third. Then the British propaganda machine kicked in, painting Thibaw as a weak drunkard, unfit for office.

In Ratnagiri, the family were then effectively kept prisoner for the following three decades. In fact, the king died and was buried there in 1916; a fact which remains controversial to this day. After his death, the queen and some of the family were quietly allowed back into Myanmar, albeit under house arrest and stripped of their titles.

But this story is not widely known in Myanmar. The British PR campaign had long-reaching implications, leaving many Burmese either unaware of, or unconcerned by, the fate of their royal family.

Interest in them has increased as the country has opened up to the world, but for Devi, it's not always welcome — unless it can help with her real cause, the environment.

"I don't want people to come and look at me like in the zoo, to see the last descendants," she says. "I want to them to accept me and love me, allow me to talk to them, based on my work."

I ask Devi if this work has ever been dangerous, or if she has ever struggled as a woman in her field. With a shrug that is becoming familiar to me as I meet more and more of these extraordinary women, she suggests not — despite the fact that being an activist of any kind under the military junta, which ruled Burma until 2011, was a risky business.

And while Devi escaped some of the horrors that faced other women in this book, her passions for the environment, democracy and peace have not come without personal cost.

She lost her job in 1988 — she was working for the government in the Department of Irrigation — because she took part in the famous anti-junta protests (for more on the '88 generation, see Chapter 4). Devi's husband, whom she met at university, worked with her but was also forced to resign after he too participated in the strike.

While Devi was at university, she had also seen her father jailed for his activism. But she says she wasn't frightened. Instead, after she lost her job, Devi opened a small shop in the house she still lives in.

"I'm not frightened, because my father trained me like an iron lady. When we resigned from our posts, I opened a shop in this place. And when my father was in jail, my mother and I opened a canteen in my school, St Mary's. And I have no shame for it," she says.

Her father is a major influence on Devi. She explains how she respects the fact that he gave up all his wealth, and his name — Taw Phaya Galay, his princely name — to become an ordinary civilian.

"He gave me lots of braveness and hardness. Whatever is coming we have to face it," says Devi.

But it was her mother who first inspired her to take up the environment as her cause. At Rangoon University, Devi was a botany major, and progressed from a Bachelor of Science to a Master of Science because of her good grades. But her father's imprisonment and the extent to which her own career was cut short meant that she ended up, as she puts it, effectively as a grocer for much of the 1990s.

"My mother said you must do something, write, write for people, to educate them. Don't just sell things here like a grocer," says Devi, touching again on the sense that — with her background — she had to do more with her life than most.

Searching for a cause, Devi turned to the books she was reading. Like many upper-class Burmese people, particularly of previous generations, Devi speaks good English and managed to access books from the West even while her country was in isolation. Increasingly, with her interest in plants, she began to see the rise of environmentalism as globally critical — and locally ignored.

"It doesn't matter if you are different colours — black, blue, brown, Christian, Muslim, Buddhist, leftist, rightist, the environment is colourless, and if it is damaged, that is very dangerous for human life," she says. "There's no east or west, we are the same, and it will affect us the same."

"So I realized, yes, I must do this for Myanmar — introduce what the environment is and how we must understand and protect it."

But Devi does not think that the environment is her duty alone. She passionately believes that ordinary people have a huge role to play, particularly in Myanmar. She is worried that decades of military rule, during which daring to put your head above the parapet about anything could get you in serious trouble (as she and her father experienced), has meant that civil society has died in Myanmar.

"People think, oh the government, they decide everything for our country. But that's wrong. For democracy — this is not the army times, this is the democratic times — the government is elected by us, so they must do what people want them to do," Devi says fiercely.

"They must listen to us. Our people should know that we are the leaders of the country."

Interest in the environment from ordinary Burmese citizens has picked up in recent years, she says, particularly following natural disasters like Cyclone Nargis, a huge storm which wreaked havoc in Myanmar in 2008 (for more on its individual impact, see Chapter 9).

"In the past, we had earthquakes, tsunamis, cyclones, but all of these were natural disasters. Why are they coming to our country with such speed now? Because these are man-made disasters," says Devi.

"We have industrial zones, we see the motorcars, they have no awareness. People using electricity, computers, not shutting them down. So we have to give lots of knowledge about that, before it's too late."

Things are improving, slowly. While Devi remains concerned that, as she puts it, "so far there are barely any rules and regulations for the environment [in Myanmar], no major environmental plan at all," there is at least now a Ministry of the Environment. It was established properly in 2011 by the former government, a military-backed civilian administration which oversaw the transition from the junta to the elections of 2015 in which Aung San Suu Kyi swept to power.

Devi has some hope that Aung San Suu Kyi, an international figure, will understand the importance of the environment and prioritize it, but she is not yet convinced by what she has seen.

Moreover, in a country riven by civil war and poverty, the environment is unlikely to reach the top of the to-do list, or even come close — although battles over natural resources are actually one of the key issues for the different ethnic armies.

The slow pace of government is one of the reasons Devi has never attempted to go into politics herself, despite people suggesting she do so for decades.

"This is the real meaning of democracy. Not going into parliament, sitting there, no talking to journalists, no interviews [Aung San Suu Kyi's party initially banned its inexperienced MPs from talking to journalists unsupervised, which sparked concerns internationally] — there are things we must do swiftly, very swiftly, like protect the Irrawaddy," says Devi.

"Time and tide wait for no man! Our Myanmar people think this is all going to be done by government. But no, first they must move by themselves and raise their voices. This is the first step," she says.

So she travels the country under her various guises giving talks and trying to inspire others, particularly the young, to care about the environment. Devi has four sons — a geologist, a businessman specializing in green tea, and two who work in digital printing — and she hopes that their generation will take on her fight for the natural world.

But it is still a tricky battle: in Myanmar many in rural areas are barely surviving, and in the urban areas others are keen to see their economy develop at any cost.

However, it's a battle that Devi is ready for. The same sense of duty that sees her polish an old painting of her ancestors with a potato to preserve it also spurs her on to keep fighting for the environment. Devi calls it her royal blood, or her sense of duty, instilled in her by her father.

"We have had difficult times in my country, and my father always taught me that we have royal blood. It is different from the civilians. We came from the ruling people, so you must always look after people. It is your duty to your country and your people," she explains.

"Don't be proud of that royal blood — you are no different to the people, you are the same as the people. But because your blood is not the same, you have a duty. So I am standing on that still now."

And despite the fact that she wants her activism to outshine her ancestry, Devi is still occasionally sad that Burmese people are barely aware of her family's continuing existence.

"In Myanmar, people don't know so much about the royal family because they are faded away, and the sunsets are long, and they think there are no descendants in Myanmar," she says.

"So I don't want to be a royal princess, but in my soul, there is one place I keep that. Once I went to the National Museum and there is a throne of my great grandfather and mother. And there were villagers there with their children and they were saying to each other how they would like to know if any descendants were alive. And oh my goodness, I am standing right there. They don't even know I am alive," she says.

But she pauses, and then seems to remember her father's teachings, and the Green Princess puts on her crown once again, which is about far, far more than recognition for her own personal background.

At the same moment, I glance over and see the book, *The King in Exile: The Fall of the Royal Family in Burma,* on her desk.

"How can I help my country, my environment, and my people? That's all," she says.

"I just want to give them [the people of Myanmar] what I can do for them."

CHAPTER SIX

The Artist: Ma Ei

TWO PEOPLE are on the stage in a gloomy performance space in downtown Yangon. One of them, the woman, has an apple, and a knife. The other, a man, has an array of make-up on a table behind him.

She starts to cut the apple and then feeds it to him. He accepts, chews, swallows. Then says, in Burmese: "I don't like apples."

He opens up one of the compacts, starts to put make-up on her.

"Make me beautiful," she tells him. "I want to be beautiful."

They go through the process again. He chews the apple. She purses her lips for the lipstick. Then they do it again. And again.

Soon, she is still feeding him apples, and by now, he is shouting about how he doesn't like apples. Meanwhile, her face is a grotesque mask of make-up: red slashes of lipstick, dark eye-shadow circles around her eyes like bruises, pancake-thick foundation. She is still asking to be made beautiful. He is still eating the apples.

The stage goes dark; the performers bow.

It's a startling, moving and powerful piece, and the audience love it. For me, it talks about human relationships, how often we don't really listen to the ones we love, and the complicated relationships between men and women in a world of outdated gender norms — men get fed, women get makeovers.

The artist behind it is Ma Ei, one of Myanmar's leading female performance artists in a vibrant modern scene.

"It is about relationships," she says afterwards. "Not only men and women but also mother and daughter, mother and son, brother and sister, friends. Sometimes we are tired of each other, but we can't stop, really, can we?" she says. She pauses, then looks up, wide-eyed, smiling. "Right?" she adds.

Ma Ei is a fascinating artist. Her work — powerful, questioning, feminist — would be ahead of the curve in any country, but in Myanmar, it's jaw-dropping. In 2015, she made headlines with an exhibition about periods, in which she lay in a red-lit room for three days and handed out sanitary towels to visitors. This, in a country where most people don't even talk about menstruation.

But despite the in-your-face, often confrontational element of much of her art, in person she is lovely; welcoming and accommodating, making coffee, juice, some food.

"I love interviews," she admits. "Because for me, I love to help somebody, I love to help you. And I like to talk about my work — the more I talk, the more I know about it."

She's talked about the controversial period piece a lot, because it drew global attention, but true-to-form, she is happy to talk about it again.

"I was planning an abstract photography exhibition, but then just before, I was with my friend. We are like brother and sister, and he was arguing with me and complaining about my work and I was really angry," she explains.

"I had my period and I was really tired, and I told him it's very painful, I have my period, but he was still arguing with me. I felt like he was abusing me. Actually it wasn't a big problem but it felt like it to me, then after when I went home, I was still feeling like, how could he not understand? He has a wife, a sister, and he still doesn't get it. I even cried that night, then I was like, ok, I have to do this."

People told her not to do it, including some senior artists, but she went ahead with the performance anyway, believing it was important to raise awareness of what women go through and often never speak about, because of the taboo in some countries like Myanmar.

"Why are we avoiding these words? We don't say them in public. But I don't care," she says. Her family didn't know about the content of the performance, other than her younger brother. However, Ma Ei thinks her mother would have approved. "She's quite an unusual mother," she says.

As Ma Ei talks more about her past, I see that she is not wrong. Growing up in the countryside outside Dawei, in the south of Myanmar, she was told by her mother that she could do anything she wanted with her life, regardless of gender. She treated Ma Ei exactly the same as she treated her brother.

"We were all just the same, she said I can do whatever I want. My mother is, like I say, special," Ma Ei says. Her mother worked as well as her father, both as small-scale traders. But her mother had had to fight for her freedom for much of her life.

"The problem is when I see other families, like my aunt and her husband. It is really awful, he points at her and says 'Hey, do that' — but she is a wife not a servant. And most of the men are like that," says Ma Ei.

"My father also took power, but my mother fought him, and got him to give her a chance and a chance for her children."

The gender imbalance left an imprint on a young Ma Ei.

"I remember my mother saying to my father once, 'Our daughter hates men, what do we do?' I thought, ooh, do I hate men? I don't know. Maybe," she says.

In some cases, she had good reason. When she was in eighth or ninth grade, she saw her mother's friends from the veranda of her house. The woman of the family was a tailor, and the family's main earner. The man spent a lot of time sitting around. But that night, just inside the couple's house, he was active: beating his wife.

"One evening I saw, he is beating her. That image is still in my head. Maybe she has forgotten, but it is still in my head," says Ma Ei.

The image has resonated with Ma Ei throughout her life.

"Oh god, it is so bad. Why is everything in my head? I don't know why. It's still there. Everybody sees those kinds of things, right? But it is only me that keeps them inside ..."

She trails off. I ask her if her art is her way of dealing with the things she has seen.

"Yes, then I express them, yes," she says. "My work is just responding to what I experience."

Since she was a little girl growing up in Dawei, those experiences have broadened considerably. She studied physics at university, a seemingly odd choice for a creative type that was dictated by the old Burmese system of allocating students a degree topic based on their matriculation marks.

She wanted to be an actress, but her boyfriend — who she is still with, thirteen years later — talked her out of it. She also hated learning the lines. She moved to Yangon to get away from the conservative society she grew up in, and after advice from one director, tried to write her own scripts.

"I said I'd try but I was lost, I didn't do anything, just watched movies and read. Then one day I tried to draw and that was the beginning of my art life!" she says, cheerfully.

Art classes followed, and then, ultimately, and after a period of hard work on the side lines, the success she now enjoys — residencies abroad (her first was in the bright lights of Tokyo, which she says was quite the shock for her first trip abroad), partnerships with galleries, acclaimed performances and exhibitions, the chance to see the world. She says her favourite artwork is Yoko Ono's dark piece, where an audience are put into a dark room, which she saw in Switzerland.

But Ma Ei's developing career in the early 2000s coincided with the peak years of Myanmar's military junta — the country's own "dark piece" — when being an artist at all was quite a brave act. She had many confrontations with the feared censorship board.

"It was a really crazy thing, and I hated it," she says. "On the first day of the opening, they come early in the morning and check every painting."

They would ask why a painting was red, the colour of Aung San Suu Kyi's National League for Democracy Party, or why it was green, the colour of soldiers.

"I once made some strokes on the canvas and they said — is it an 8? Oh no! Hell! They thought it was like the '88 generation [huge protests in 1988 which were ultimately crushed but launched a new generation of activists and dissidents, including Aung San Suu Kyi]. But I swear it wasn't, it was just some strokes," says Ma Ei.

However, at other times, she found them easy to fool about her intentions.

"I did some photo art about politics — I made a Photoshop of a spider web, and I was sitting in front of the web, you know, with no freedom. And they came to check and asked me what it was about and I said, oh, Buddhism, and they believed me!" she says, going off into peals of her unexpectedly dirty-sounding laughter. "I tricked them — I was a good liar!"

Still, it wasn't an ideal situation to be an artist.

"It's much easier now," Ma Ei admits. But then she laughs again, and her tone turns mocking.

"Yeah, we are all feeling much better now. I'm not angry anymore, I'm totally fine now," she says, her voice sarcastic.

She's joking, but she has a serious point. While things are improving in now semi-democratic Myanmar, Ma Ei still has questions — and the country still has a long way to go.

"Maybe now they are not so much about politics; now they are about life, our world, our universe," she says.

And, of course, she has questions about the treatment of women in Myanmar.

"It is an unfair place," she says. "Why? For example, in the morning, when you go to the market, who is buying the groceries? A woman. And when you look at the teashop at the same time, most of the people there are men, sitting, reading journals, talking about the football match. This is morning, and night also. They watch football, the women are ironing, cleaning. A women's daily life is about work for the house — and even if they both have a job, the woman does the housework and the man just relaxes."

In Ma Ei's own domestic set-up, it's not quite the same — she and her long-term boyfriend live apart, because she says she loves her own space, and they have no children — and she goes to her family home around the corner for meals every day. But despite the emancipation of her own mother, it is still her mum who cooks the family's food every day, since moving to Yangon a few years after Ma Ei.

Can things change, for her mother, and for other women in Myanmar?

"No, I don't think so, not yet," says Ma Ei. "All of the women have to know that it's unfair, but most of them don't know that yet, they think it's their duty. That's the problem."

Although she would find it a slightly reductive label, raising awareness, then, is part of what her work is about. She certainly doesn't think art should always be beautiful — "sometimes art should be ugly" — she says — but she believes it should always make people think, like the period piece.

"Art can change things, but it will take time. I want it to stay in their mind, maybe they will change later. I want people to go away thinking, especially the men — the society — I want them to think if society is treating women fairly or not," she says.

This inquiring approach can mean her work is seen as confrontational. She once cooked noodles in front of a crowd dressed in a male *longyi* (as we've explored elsewhere, clothes are a big deal in Myanmar — men and women's clothes aren't supposed to mix, even in the washing, and many believe that for a man to even touch a women's clothing is to lose his male power). Another time, she painted the nails of a male audience member.

"Most of my work is asking questions," she says. "Questioning gender even — why? What is man? What has made this situation?"

Sometimes that also means asking questions of herself.

"I had an exhibition once with the name, Who am I? People call me Ma Ei, but it's just a name, this piece of meat, this combination of flesh and bone, what is this?" she says.

She also thinks it's important to question value: while a diamond is valuable to a human, it is worthless to a monkey, she says. Spiky comments like this, alongside her often challenging work, would lead many in Myanmar to consider her an "angry young woman" — if such a concept had spread here — but now thirty-nine-year-old Ma Ei herself thinks she is more inquisitive than anything.

"I just don't understand all of this. The value thing, the period thing, I don't understand people and society, so that's why [I ask these questions]," she says.

However, she admits that there is some anger lying behind her work, as anyone watching the first piece I saw, with the apples, would understand.

"Yeah I suppose — I don't understand things, and then that makes me a little bit angry," she says.

Channelling her anger into her work is also no doubt helped by her hobby of meditation, allowing her to focus on the here and now when things get too much. She doesn't meditate every day, but says that most of the time she tries to concentrate on what she has doing in a mindful manner.

"So you know, every movement — what are you doing?" she says. "It makes me very peaceful, when I just concentrate on the air, on breathing, if I really concentrate, I can forget everything."

She says meditation is a hobby rather than part of her religious faith, although she is a Buddhist. In Buddhism, she finds a place where there are no questions.

"Buddhism is not about questions, I am quite sure," she says. "My favourite work I have done is called Endless. It is a photography series, performative photography. It is supposed to be like my funeral. I lie on the floor and we put some flowers, different colours of flowers on my body. This is my endless series — I want to say we have a long life, but we are passing through one life after another, many lives."

This idea of reincarnation is central in Buddhism, and it is one which appeals to Ma Ei very much.

"I believe," she says simply. "I believe that what we have is what we did in the past. Because why are some people very rich, some poor, some beautiful, some ugly? I learned what I learned from physics — I always say it is about energy. Energy cannot be created, it cannot be destroyed. We are running by some kind of energy, so when we die, it is only the body — the energy cannot die. So it transforms into another life," she says.

She adds cheerfully that I can disagree, but her belief comes from

Buddhism and science together, so it is pretty strong, and then she heads to the kitchen to make a mango juice. It's hot season and there's a power cut, taking her air conditioning out of action, and we are stifling even in her roomy, high-up apartment.

She keeps talking from the kitchen, where the walls have pictures of kittens rather than her own work. She says her only quarrel with Buddhism is how it is used unfairly by society to discriminate against women.

"They say a woman's body is a dirty thing, but society did that. Buddha didn't say that — what he says is practical, not superstitious. I am really happy to explain this to foreigners because this is very stupid," she says.

She's also happy to explain to me the paintings and photographs on the wall (her own mainly, including some beautiful works that are close-up photographs of the balls used to hold moisture in plants), her vast DVD collection ("I love movies"), the bottles of pills on the table next to us (a vitamin D deficiency) and the huge purple teddy bear sitting on her sofa like a friend.

"It's part of my artwork. I did a performance with many teddy bears and other toys, I sat in the middle of it for two hours — still, like them," she says. "I didn't even blink."

And despite her candour throughout our conversation, she's a bit more coy when I ask her what made her an artist. At first she just laughs, and says it's a big question. But her open nature wins out in the end, and she tries to answer this huge existential poser as best she can.

"When I was a child, I was just a stupid child, very quiet. But even since then I have this feeling — I don't know how to say — I felt like I am an artist," she says.

She says she notices things others do not — both good and bad — and holds on to them, as she mentioned before, often wanting to make them more visible.

"I remember in the compound of our house, there were many plants there and I saw these tiny flowers," she says.

"And they were so beautiful, and I thought, do people not notice that? I can make a picture of that."

CHAPTER SEVEN

The Refugee Sexual Health Nurse: Mu Tha Paw

THERE IS a persistent Western myth that the Burmese language has no word for vagina. It's a convenient symbol for journalists, often used to represent Myanmar's sexual repression and lack of reproductive rights for women.

Unfortunately for the neatness of the analogy, the myth is not true. There are direct translations for vagina in Burmese and in many of Myanmar's other languages. And in rapidly developing, worldly Yangon, sex is often on show: condoms are on sale in some corner shops, some bold young women have started to dress as sexily as they like, and couples canoodle under strategically placed umbrellas at sunset by Kandawgi lakeside.

There's a dark side to this too; there are brothels in many towns, and even so-called tinsel bars, where men pick their women by throwing strings of glittery paper around their necks and paying for their time and "attention".

However, none of this means that talking about sex in this country is easy.

Mu Tha Paw is thirty-four years old. She is Karen, part of an ethnic group who live mainly in Myanmar and Thailand. They have a different language, traditions, and even dress than the ethnic Bamar people who make up around 70 per cent of Myanmar's population.

And the Karen approach to sex is about as taboo as it gets. While the Karen language does have a word for vagina — *poe tha klayi*, which literally means "the way that the baby comes out" — it's basically unmentionable, rarely used even in a family or health setting.

That's why it's a shock to hear Mu Tha Paw breezily talking about vaginal exams, IUDs and the contraceptive implant (often using the English terms) within two minutes of sitting down next to me, in a bamboo-shack café on the roadside next to Mae La refugee camp in Thailand.

But then, Mu Tha Paw is no ordinary woman. She is a sexual health nurse and a refugee, one of hundreds of thousands of Karen who fled war in their homeland of Myanmar, and she has trained herself out of embarrassment because she wants to help other women.

"That word is not a polite word to say," she explains. "Most Karen women and girls are so embarrassed to say it."

But for her, it's no biggie. Unfortunately, that's not quite the case for our translator, a college student who also lives in the camp, who we have to cajole into saying the word either in Karen or English.

He makes it in the end, after an hour or so of intense coaching from Mu Tha Paw, as we pick at noodles and crisps, wafting away insects, in the shade of the thatched roof by the camp.

Afterwards, he tells me his girlfriend (also a refugee) lives in America now, and so he has to get used to other cultures than his own. He knows she wears a bikini on the beach in Los Angeles, and he is okay with it, because that's the way things are in other countries.

Mu Tha Paw nods approvingly when this statement is translated back into Karen. She thinks the stigma around talking about sex is risking people's lives — many of the refugee women who come to see her are too embarrassed to talk about their bodies and their problems, sometimes until it is too late.

"The first time I talk to them, it's the first time they have ever talked about family planning or reproductive health," she says. "People don't talk about it."

In Mu Tha Paw's home community, back in a small town in a rural area of Karen state, this meant that sex education, family planning, sexual health services and supplies were at a very low level. Some villages use a kind of herb to try to prevent pregnancy, and only really stop having children when they are old.

This is not unusual. Abortion is illegal in Myanmar unless the woman's life is at risk, sexual education in schools is unheard of, and according to Marie Stopes International, only one in three women in the country uses any kind of modern contraception. The problem is exacerbated in rural and remote areas, for low-income women, and — of course — for refugees, who have other battles to fight, from basic survival upwards.

"It's often all secret," says Mu Tha Paw. "Some people like condoms, some don't, but it's kept secret. When we go to their houses, sometimes people are shy. We have to go slowly, slowly, so people can decide for themselves that this is an ok thing."

For Mu Tha Paw and her team in Mae La camp, that means sometimes literally going door-to-door on the hillside. They aren't visiting tents: Mae La camp was established in 1984, and its inhabitants now live in huts of varying levels of permanence. It's basically a town, with all of the facilities a town would need — apart from that its residents are not really allowed to leave, and face arrest by the Thai police if they try.

It is the biggest of nine refugee camps on the Thai-Burma border, which house more than 100,000 refugees between them, according to the United Nations.

The camps were set up in response to the huge numbers of civilians who were forced to flee Myanmar over the last thirty years to escape death, torture, rape, landmines and forced labour at the hands of the Burmese military regime.

The civilians were caught up in a fierce ethnic conflict between the Karen National Union (KNU) — who were fighting for autonomy for their region in the south of Myanmar — and the fearsome Burmese army, the Tatmadaw. The battle had been raging for decades. In fact, it was routinely known as the longest-running civil war in the world, and had been ongoing since Myanmar won its independence from the British colonial power in 1948.

A historic ceasefire was initially agreed in 2012, after the generals handed over power to a military-backed civilian administration in 2011, marking the beginning of changes in Myanmar. A further wide-ranging peace deal was signed in 2015 alongside a number of other rebel groups, although some fighting continues.

But the uneasy and partial peace after decades of war has still left hundreds of thousands of Karens displaced, including Mu Tha Paw. She left Myanmar in 2006, aged just twenty-four. She was alone and frightened, but she had no choice.

"When I lived there, I heard guns every day," she says. "I came here because of the wars. We had no business, we could do nothing. There was a siege, and then there was no rice. I had nothing."

Life was difficult for both sexes at that time, Mu Tha Paw recalls; while many men were on the battlefield, an altogether more sordid war faced many of the women. As we've seen elsewhere in this book, rape is still used as a weapon of war in a number of conflicts across Myanmar.

"There was a lot of violence against women," says Mu Tha Paw, who seems uneasy for the only time in our conversation. This isn't surprising: rape is still among the least discussed topics in her culture, regardless of her role, and there's the double whammy in this situation of accusing the feared and fierce Tatmadaw, who still act almost with impunity in Myanmar despite the country's transition to a semi-democratic state.

"They killed women, there was sexual violence, it was very dangerous for women," she whispers.

The situation has, at least on paper, improved for the Karen since the ceasefire in 2015. In fact, there's even talk of some of the refugees returning home — although many are understandably frightened about doing so.

Myanmar's new figurehead, Aung San Suu Kyi, has made finding a lasting peace one of her top priorities (unfortunately, it's not going too well — ethnic conflicts have flared up across the country in recent months, arguably a sign of her government's continued lack of power over the military). Mu Tha Paw isn't convinced either.

"I never hope she can help," she says. Instead, Mu Tha Paw and thousands like her — some of whom have spent decades in the camps

— have taken it into their own hands to try and improve their lives, even while their futures hang in the balance.

For Mu Tha Paw, that means working hard in her chosen career.

"[Traditionally], we don't have knowledge, and we don't talk about this [sex]," she says. "But we can help them with all of their problems."

Mu Tha Paw and her colleagues at the family planning clinic in Mae La camp were trained by the Planned Parenthood Association of Thailand (supported by the United Nations Population Fund). Executive director Montri Pekanan said the impetus came from the women themselves — women like Mu Tha Paw.

"Helping them to take control of their fertility helps them to take control of their lives," he tells me by phone from Bangkok.

The programme began back in 2000, and now operates across five refugee camps. The family planning services have reached an estimated 73,000 women, and the sexual and reproductive health education programme has reached another 4,200 women.

They provide advice, medicine, condoms, the pill, IUDs, and the contraceptive implant, as well as support for pregnant women and consultations on other reproductive health issues and hygiene. For serious problems, they refer the women to a hospital either in the camp or in the nearby city of Mae Sot. The nurses earn 2,200 baht (roughly £43) a month.

At first, people were suspicious of the new services; husbands thought their wives would be unfaithful, parents thought it would encourage premarital sex, a taboo in the mainly Christian community, and some even thought it was a ploy to control refugee numbers. However, because the nurses come from within the community, these fears have been assuaged. Pekanan said the nurses have become motivators, figureheads for the other women in the camp.

It's a role that Mu Tha Paw, who is married and has a seven-year-old son, takes seriously. Wearing the pink T-shirt of the scheme, joking with me about the spicy food, I can see how her warm manner puts women at ease. She has been working as a nurse for nine years, since a year or so after her arrival in the camp.

"I said I'd like to do this, as a woman I wanted to learn about children and to know more about health, how to prevent sickness and problems, and help other people," she says.

She says sexual and reproductive health are discussed so little in her community that she thought she was dying the first time she got her period — something she doesn't want other young Karen girls to go through.

"I felt in danger and scared. I did not know what was happening," she says.

"And then when I had a baby — the pain, and I knew nothing. Now I know more."

She says it is not an overstatement to say that, in her area of Myanmar during the war, there was no sexual education or awareness at all.

"In Burma, we didn't have family planning. We did not know anything about how to stop children, help with problems," she says. "Now we have modern medicine."

Since she began the job, she thinks she has helped many women — and for her it is more than just a health issue. It's a way of helping women take control of their own destinies, in a small way.

"Women here are so busy, their lives are so difficult. But their husbands don't want to think about the wife's health. No, the only thing the husband thinks about is his wife's body, not how she feels about having a baby," says Mu Tha Paw, fiercely.

"We think if the wife decides to stop having babies, there is nothing the husband can do about it."

It's not a problem in her own family, she laughs — her husband is very happy with her work and her knowledge. They would like to have another child if they can, and Mu Tha Paw wants a daughter.

But while she is an inspiring and cheerful figure, it's hard to forget that Mu Tha Paw is a refugee, unwelcome in Thailand, unsafe in her own country, and unable to leave. Foreign journalists aren't even allowed in the camp to see the conditions there, and we only get close by keeping our presence quiet.

"If I want to go outside, I cannot, so this is a problem," frowns Mu Tha Paw. And it gets worse. At the moment, her husband is not working.

"We have many problems: to pay the fees for the children's school, even just to get breakfast. It's always about money. We only have 100 baht (about US$3) left," she says.

Her future remains uncertain, as it is unclear what will happen — funding for the camps or for relocations to countries like the United States have both dwindled since the ceasefires, but at the same time, many Karen, including Mu Tha Paw, do not feel safe going back to their country. Among other things, they fear the landmines that both sides undoubtedly left strewn around the landscape (Myanmar has one of the worst rates of landmine deaths in the world).

Going back would be a struggle anyway: Mu Tha Paw and her husband have no land in Myanmar, and no house — and no money to obtain them.

But whatever happens, Mu Tha Paw says she plans to keep working in sexual health, helping Karen women to open their minds and, with that, open up their possibilities.

"I give women power by giving them knowledge," she says, simply.

CHAPTER EIGHT

The Rohingya and Human Rights Champion: Wai Wai Nu

IN 2005, when Wai Wai Nu was eighteen, she was arrested and put in prison by Burma's generals for no other reason than that her father was an opposition member of parliament (MP). Unfazed, she sassed the judge and reassured her family even as she was taken behind bars.

When she was released seven years later, undaunted and even inspired by the injustice she had both suffered and seen in jail, she immediately began work as a human rights and women's rights activist.

When I first met her in 2015, she was busy campaigning for equal human rights for all, despite the shadowy presence of Special Branch police officers haunting the events she spoke at.

In short, I think she might be one of the gutsiest people I have ever met.

Now, though — as we talk at the end of 2017 — the thirty-one-year-old is wary. She speaks diplomatically, thoughtfully, and she is obviously worried about the topics we discuss over the phone as she heads to visit her father in hospital in Bangkok.

That's because she is also a Rohingya Muslim, a member of an ethnic group in Myanmar who have been called the most persecuted in the world.

In recent months, an unimaginably brutal campaign of violence against the Rohingya in their home state of Rakhine has seen around 700,000 flee the country.

Thousands have been killed, many of the women gang raped, and hundreds of their home villages burnt by the Burmese army. The UN's top human rights official has said it looks like possible genocide — a genocide that is, almost unthinkably, being overseen by the government of Nobel Peace Prize laureate Aung San Suu Kyi.

For Wai Wai Nu, it's even closer to home. Her eighty-seven-year-old grandma has been displaced by the violence. Her house, land and village have all been destroyed, and she is currently in Buthidaung, a town in Rakhine, because she cannot walk to Bangladesh. She has no one to help her. Wai Wai's family in Myanmar cannot reach her.

"She has lost everything," says Wai Wai Nu, who struggles to find the words to describe what is happening in Myanmar.

"It is unbelievable. The UN is saying this is ethnic cleansing, crimes against humanity, even genocide. I can't believe that it is happening in my country, before my eyes — a beautiful country, with kind-hearted people, a just society. But now you can see the gravity, the scale, the scope of the condition. It is really unacceptable. It's just ... it's horrific."

Sadly, it's not without precedent in Myanmar. Waves of violence, often state-sponsored and led by the army, have rolled in on the Rohingya several times in recent decades. After a particularly serious set of clashes in 2012 (because, while the retribution has been disproportionate, there have been attacks by Rohingya on the predominantly Buddhist Rakhinese community that they live alongside too), around 150,000 were put in camps for the internally displaced persons (IDPs) in Rakhine — and they have not been allowed to leave since.

Until recently, about 1 million Rohingya lived in Myanmar, and those outside the camps hardly had a much better time. Routinely abused by police, their movements were restricted, their ID cards removed, and they were disenfranchised in the 2015 elections. But that pales into insignificance compared to what they are currently facing.

For Wai Wai, the violence has a depressingly familiar ring to it — and particularly in one of the grimmest elements: the old Tatmadaw tactic, as we saw in Chapter 2, of using rape as a weapon of war, targeting women in particular n their campaign of fear.

Wai Wai Nu says the fact that there has been absolutely no retribution for this despite evidence of attacks from many different ethnic conflicts, over many decades, has encouraged the army to continue to act with impunity.

"When this crisis happened, I couldn't believe that rape was still being used so systematically to really traumatize and dehumanize the population. It's such a scary thing — how dare they?" says Wai Wai Nu.

What she wants now is some action to help the Rohingya, and it's an issue she has raised where she can in meetings and advocacy in recent months outside Myanmar, although she is reluctant to go into detail too much (drawing attention to yourself as a Rohingya campaigner is unwise if you want to have a future inside Myanmar). And Wai Wai Nu does want that future, and, in the long-term, she also wants justice for her people — and acceptance of their right to be in Myanmar.

"When it comes to crimes against humanity, there has to be justice," she says simply. "It is hard to compensate for the suffering and the loss. We cannot even measure what justice can compensate for this. But something has to happen. I don't know if it will or not, but I strongly believe it has to happen."

Wai Wai Nu knows a thing or two about justice. A lawyer by training, she is currently studying at Berkeley in the United States for a postgraduate law degree.

She says it has been hard for her not to be in Myanmar in recent months, because she feels useless. But there's another side to it as well: the media's insistence on portraying her as some kind of Rohingya poster girl.

"First of all, I am a Rohingya and I want to be a Rohingya, but I don't just want to be a Rohingya," says Wai Wai Nu. "I want to be a human rights and women's rights activist, a person who believes in humanity, I don't want to be portrayed in the box. It gives a chance to society to exclude me, creates a misunderstanding with the public in Burma, and I feel so much pressure."

And it is unfairly reductive to only talk to Wai Wai Nu about the plight of her people, as her work is so much wider than that — taking in peace building, women, youth, and other minorities.

"As a Rohingya I have to speak and not just because I am a Rohingya. It's because I stand for the weak and all minorities," she says.

But Wai Wai Nu's opinions on the matter haven't stopped the headlines; the one which annoys her the most is probably *The Daily Beast*'s decision in 2016 to christen her the "Rohingya Princess", a wildly inappropriate title even at the time, considering the suffering faced by most Rohingya.

(As an aside, why are high-achieving women still called princesses in this day and age? It's rare to see powerful men called princes. I wonder if this is because the idea of a man reaching the top is less of a fairy tale).

In fact, she's even less keen on her nickname than the Green Princess, Devi Thant Cin, who we met a few chapters ago and who at least has her bloodline to blame.

In one of our early meetings, I teased Wai Wai Nu about her meteoric rise to royalty.

"Agh, please," she responded dismissively. "This is crazy."

On the one hand, you can see where *The Daily Beast* was trying to go. With a bit of poetic licence, you could argue that Wai Wai Nu was imprisoned by evil overlords; she does provide hope for her people, although she does much more than that; and she is both brave and beautiful.

Her prison was no mythical castle, surrounded by spiky vines and ogres, though. Instead she was in Yangon's notorious Insein jail, put there by Myanmar's generals, which is about as far from fairy tales as you can get.

And while her role as a figure of hope for her people might piss her off, she does accept it. Her bravery, as I've said, is also clearly apparent, and she is beautiful — although I wouldn't tell her to her face, because until we've met a few times, I am a little scared of Wai Wai. I see her again and again at rallies and peace events she has organized, write about her a few times, chat with her in various places, but never seem to break through to the person beneath the amazing, but slightly intimidating, human rights icon.

I later realize this is out-of-character, because as I get to know her properly, I see she is warm and kind, incredibly focused on helping people and making a difference, and very open — with a mischievous sense of humour to boot. Later in our relationship, she bullies me (gently) into teaching a volunteer English class at her organization, buys me thoughtful presents from her trips away, and laughs a lot.

I think the initial problem is that she is simply too busy: running from one person to the next, setting up the next event, talking to the next media organization. She says her family and friends, when she manages to see them, constantly urge her to take a holiday (I soon become one of these people, telling her she must take a break), but she simply has too much to do. In fact, when I ask about friends, she says she barely has time for them either — most of her friends are activists like her. And she wouldn't have time to see them anyway — she hasn't really had a day off since she was released from prison six years ago.

It's not hard to see why: as well as raising her causes internationally (most recently, at the UN in Geneva, taking part in panels on women's rights, youth rights and minority rights), she has a number of other roles. She is the co-founder of Women for Justice and the founder and director of the Women Peace Network Arakan (Arakan is the old term for Rakhine), civil society organizations in Yangon.

The organizations train people, particularly women, and empower others to support human rights in Myanmar — from political training to peace-building. They also work with government and international organizations where possible, from the UN down, on reporting and drafting new policies on Myanmar, and particularly on Rakhine and the Rohingya. The latter also provides free or almost-free English classes to young people.

"Most of my time is spent with them [Women Peace Network Arakan]. It's under the Yangon Youth Center so it's meant for young people, but anyone can join — man, woman, Buddhist, Christian, Muslim, whoever," she says.

It's not a small commitment.

"Often the teachers are volunteers, they just come personally to help me, because they see this is important and they are passionate about it. So whenever I am not travelling I am there," says Wai Wai.

In the last few years, she has also spearheaded the "My Friend" campaign, which took off internationally. The idea was to encourage young people from different religious or ethnic backgrounds to take selfies together, and post them online with the hashtag #myfriend.

In a country with the background of Myanmar outlined above, this message of tolerance and friendship was huge. Thousands have taken part in the campaign, posting photos on Facebook with heartfelt messages like: "Our religion is different, our ethnicity is different, but we are friends and we love each other."

It's a beautiful story among a darker role for Facebook in Myanmar, which has also become a platform for hate speech and abuse as social media use has rocketed in the rapidly liberalizing country.

"We have to make sure young people are not engaging with this. We want young people to use social media in an effective way for society," says Wai Wai Nu.

Moreover, harnessing people power in this way, as well as utilizing the loudspeaker effect of social media, is important for Wai Wai's work, because activism doesn't come cheap. Her efforts are funded partly by her family's own money, partly by the community, and partly by grants, although she doesn't want to go into the grant side of things because she says local people can see grants as unwanted international interfering. She hopes the new government will soon begin to allocate money to supporting civil society, but at the moment there's no sign of this.

For this reason, at the moment, campaigns and organizations like #myfriend will continue to rely on the almost complete dedication of people like Wai Wai. It's a big ask. I wonder if it is something she ever thought she would pledge her life to in such an all-encompassing way.

"I never imagine that I would be as busy as this," she says. "Not since I was released from jail in 2012 have I ever taken a holiday. I work like this all day, until late at night."

There's a glimpse of the young woman that Wai Wai still is when she admits she doesn't like getting up early in the morning, and another glimpse of the world in which she operates when she confesses that her dedication has caused her some problems in her own family: she still lives with her parents and some of her siblings in downtown Yangon.

"My mum is like — you are always working, you are out of the family," she says. "She was kind of joking because I can't help her as a woman — you know, in our culture you have to help your mum at home and I can't help at all, and she was like, you're useless!"

Her mum has since realized that Wai Wai is far from useless, although both of her parents still worry about how much danger she is in as an activist, even under the new regime. Her particular focus on two contentious topics — women's rights and Rohingya rights — only makes it worse.

Wai Wai Nu isn't exaggerating, either. When I attend some of her events, I see Special Branch loitering, waiting for her to push it too far.

"When I started activism, my dad did not agree. Because I am a woman, he is worried that it is dangerous work, and also that people will gossip. Also he was protective — he didn't want his daughter to face the same experiences he had. But he couldn't stop me," says Wai Wai.

He changed his opinion after his daughter aced some political skills training in Chiang Mai, Thailand — long a location for Burmese dissidents — in 2012, soon after her release from jail.

"He realized I could do it and he didn't stop me anymore. That was a cool thing," she says.

It is important for Wai Wai to have the support of her parents, because despite the fact that she is a now a famous woman comfortable championing her causes across the world, who has met former U.S. President Barack Obama, among others, and whose opinion is taken seriously at the highest levels, she is still living under their roof and abiding by their rules.

While they are now proud of her achievements — she recently added the accolade of being voted one of *Time*'s Next Generation Leaders to her roster of plaudits awarded by everyone from the BBC to the Nobel Women's Initiative — Wai Wai is expected to respect her elders.

Doing so is part of her Muslim background, as are her attempts to pray as often as she can.

"This is our culture. Before you get married, you cannot live separately," she says. "I love living with my family, they are strict but they do allow me to do what I want to do."

Wai Wai, like many other unmarried Burmese girls of her age, has a curfew of 7 p.m. or 8 p.m. at the latest. She's also likely to have an arranged marriage.

For a Western woman about the same age, I find the curfew — and the idea of arranged marriage — strange and restrictive. Wai Wai understands, but explains the reasoning behind it.

"It's cultural. Also, since I became well known, it's not safe, with the work I am doing [to be out late]," she says. "Also it doesn't look in the community. In our culture women are supposed to stay at home, always be nice, things like that."

She understands why this upsets women's rights advocates from other cultures, and admits it upsets her too. But she explains that the curfew has to be seen in the context of wider Myanmar and the relative lack of safety for some women.

"Of course I believe that women should be allowed out whenever they want, and there should be a secure environment for women, like having rule of law and respect for women's dignity," she says.

"But it's not always easy to go against your culture, or your family rules, because you love your family."

It's a nuanced take on a tricky topic, and there's another similar issue that Wai Wai often has to confront. As pop star Ah Moon has experienced (see Chapter 10), as well as not going where they want, when they want, Burmese women are also restricted in wearing what they want to wear. Many still wear the traditional *htamein*, a sarong-like covering that is the sister of the male *longyi*, and otherwise dress conservatively.

"I think again it is an issue of balance," says Wai Wai, who mainly chooses to wear traditional dress. "Because you're staying in this society. You know, when you try to change society, you need to make it a little bit strategic, otherwise you will become an enemy of society.

"I personally believe women should be able to wear whatever they want, of course — but you need to be able to wear just a little bit of the culture too."

Basically, she thinks there are bigger fights than clothing, so she fights those. Also, she likes Burmese dress, and that's understandable: it is historic, it is unique, and it's also beautiful and practical, often in jewelled colours and gorgeous patterns, in light fabrics that cover vulnerable limbs from the fierce sun.

But she does see the fight about clothing, and indeed curfews, as skirmishes which represent the wider battle that women not just in Myanmar, but globally, must take on.

"If you don't maintain your culture, then you are the enemy of it — and in particular this burden to maintain culture and religion is on women," she says.

"But why should women have to carry the burden of maintaining culture and other things, religion and more, and why not men? I had this fight with my brother the other day, and he cannot answer me."

And really, that's the root of the problem, she argues; it's at the heart of why Myanmar is not a fair society for women.

"Society is trying to make women guilty because you don't maintain your culture. This is not fair, it should be with the consent of its women. So it's not just about the clothing in Myanmar. It's more about attitude; and mostly, the attitude towards women here is still very discriminatory, still with male domination."

She says that both men and women cling to what she sees as outdated and unfair attitudes to women in Myanmar.

"Women have to be polite, to be nice, to be quiet. Why? Why do you see women as a subject who has to do whatever you want her to do? If women go outside now the sexual harassment is very common — visual, verbal, even physical. It's …" she sighs, and pauses.

"We have a long way to go."

One of the things that makes her the most angry about attitudes towards women in Myanmar is that many people don't think anything is wrong — a sentiment shared by some of the other women in this book.

"It's really funny that they try to pretend, oh no, we respect the women, the mothers are the most valuable and respected in the family. But what if she goes out? Right. She may not get the same respect. So there's a long way to go not just in attitude change but in structural change, in terms of women's rights, to be able to walk freely, do whatever they want freely, sit in parliament.

"There's so much to do and I think in terms of security, particularly in rural areas and conflict areas, women are still living in fear of threat — physical, mental, sexual. So it's a big area."

And for Wai Wai Nu, who has said in the past that prison was her university, women's rights are an area she first truly learned about while she was in jail. Her previous life — in Rakhine, which at that time was not segregated, so she faced very little discrimination for her religion or ethnicity, and later in Yangon — did not teach her about the injustice that was rife across her nation.

"When I was young, I never thought I would be standing as a women's rights activist or a feminist," she says. "Then when we were in jail, I was surprised to see so many women — about 150 — in there too, and the majority were young women, and I was really upset about this."

At first, she didn't dare to speak to them. But then she did, and as she talked to these women, she realized that others had different crosses to bear than her own.

"I realized I am interested in people's lives, particularly single women. I talked a lot with these women from different backgrounds, a lot of prostitutes, about why they had to do this, what is there hope, and I learned a lot from them," she says.

Her initial months in prison were a huge challenge, she admits, battling the anger of why she had been imprisoned without a fair trial, a law student aged only eighteen.

"I was so upset, I thought I have lost everything. I have no hope anymore. So it was really difficult for me to survive," she says.

But then her conversations with women who she says were in an even darker place than her helped her realize what she had to do.

"But then after I talked to these women, one by one, I feel that there is still some hope, I realize I am so lucky, because I know what's going on with my own life," she says.

"Whereas these women don't know what's happening to them, how to get what they want. There were only a few women in that jail — whether it was gambling or theft, or prostitution — who were working with their own consent. The vast majority didn't want it at all.

"I really learned from them. They didn't want to do this but they are here and I realized it is because of the country's political system, the economic system, and the culture. It's not their fault. And I don't want to see this anymore."

It would be tempting to use this story as a moment of redemption, Shawshank-style, proving that good triumphs over evil even in the worst of circumstances, giving Wai Wai purpose in her darkest hours.

She admits that would be tempting for her too, but in reality the seven long years she spent in prison were far darker than this.

"Of course I have mental trauma," she says. In particular, she says it was difficult for her to think of other young people out in the world, doing things, making change happen, while she was stuck in her cell.

"I am useless, I am just in prison, I cannot do anything," she remembers. "I was crying in my heart, and it was difficult to overcome — unfortunately you don't have anything to help you overcome trauma in prison. So I tried to do it myself by reading books, by keeping hope, by talking to women."

I ask her how often she is haunted by the huge chunk of time she spent behind bars.

"I don't think of it every day, but when I have interviews and people ask, the pain — it's painful to think about it again. But then I feel more dedicated in fighting injustice, because I don't want other youths or women to feel like this," she says.

"It will be in my heart forever, that pain. It's difficult to recover, because although you forgive someone or get justice — and I don't think we have justice — I don't think it will lead to recovery. We were treated badly, like criminals by the prison staff, locked in our cells, forced to do work, screamed at."

Jail time of this type is a spectre that haunts an entire generation of Burmese activists, from Aung San Suu Kyi down. The Lady, as she is fondly known in Myanmar, famously spent fifteen years under house arrest. She was just one of thousands of activists routinely imprisoned on spurious charges and kept behind bars for decades under the power of the military junta.

For her part, Wai Wai Nu remembers the day she and her family were sentenced. She was a student at Yangon East University.

"You know, before I went to jail, I was just a student, I wasn't that involved in politics," she says.

"Then we are in court and the judge is looking at me, and as she was reading from the paper, sentencing us, without any sympathy, I said: 'Thank you so much for your sentence, don't worry, we should be fine.' And I turned to my dad and said, 'Dad, you know our grandma is still alive at ninety-nine years so don't worry, you'll be fine,'" she says, with a fair amount of sass.

In those touchy days, this could have easily seen a few more years slapped onto her sentence. But Wai Wai didn't care then, and doesn't care now.

"I'm not brave. It's just because I was not guilty, I didn't do anything, I feel like there is no point putting us in jail. This is ridiculous, and unacceptable. I was so angry," she says.

Her resistance continued as she was taken to jail, with her mother and sister. All prisoners have to sit down with crossed arms, and Wai Wai refused to sit like this.

"The highest prison officer, very threatening, came to me and asked why I was not doing it, and asking me what I was charged for. And I said I didn't know. I said: 'I don't know why I have been charged, or why I have this sentence, because I have done nothing. And if you want to know, go and ask the court,'" says Wai Wai.

It was impossibly daring.

"It was the first day," laughs Wai Wai. "And she was already so upset at me that no one even dared look at her. She told the junior officers, take them out of my sight!"

The bravado didn't go unpunished. Wai Wai and her sister were taken to a separate wing and left alone, ignored by the guards other than to be watched over. Her family were very nervous, and in the first investigation, her mother's small amount of cash was stripped from her. It had been the only way the family were able to get food.

"So we have nothing to eat and we lost all our little things and my mum started to cry," remembers Wai Wai. Luckily, the head of the women's ward in the prison heard of how they were being treated, and gave them some food and a better place to live in the prison, in line with other political prisoners.

"These officers, they are awful. They don't respect human dignity at all. To other women, they were always treating us inhumanely, shouting, yelling, beating. I realized this is because of the training they get, the impunity they feel, the structures of this corrupted country," says Wai Wai.

Wai Wai and her family were eventually released in 2012. The generals who had ruled the country for decades had relinquished their grip on power — in part — the preceding year, transitioning to a military-backed civilian government that, while it continued to have many problems, did at least begin to liberalize Myanmar to an extent.

"I feel like the regime totally ignored the people of this country. I used to imagine while I was in prison, what if I was their daughter? Would they do this? No," says Wai Wai.

"But they were completely different, ignorant, disrespectful dictators. So I didn't know how to understand the conditions I was facing, and I always thought how could they do this to their family? But they don't think like that, they just put you in jail.

"They were always trying to claim they were the protectors of the state, but it's not true."

Wai Wai remembers the day of freedom "like a dream", with her dad arriving at the family house later as he was in a prison in another part of the country.

"I just walked out with my family. I didn't — I couldn't believe it was really happening. Then we went home to Tamwe [an area in Yangon], and we were waiting for my dad. He came at midnight and we realized this is really happening. It was unbelievable," she says.

But she is aghast that, five years later, there are still political prisoners in Myanmar's jails.

The military-backed government, led by the Union Solidarity and Development Party (USDP) that freed her family, didn't make enough effort to free others, says Wai Wai — and continued to imprison dissidents. But more importantly, she wants to see more from Aung San Suu Kyi, the most famous political prisoner in Myanmar's history.

"I hope they do not forget the suffering of people, and they try to change," she says.

"So I welcome the release of student activists we have seen, and I also want to see the release of people who are in prison without a fair trial, whether they are political prisoners or not — there are a lot of people just accused and put in for anything they want. The prostitutes, I don't want to see them in prison, they need a proper system to recover their lives and protect them."

However, in recent months, her hopes on this front have started to fade. For example, literary freedom of speech network PEN Myanmar says at least thirty-eight people have been charged with online defamation since April 2016 (when the new government took power). That's under the notorious Article 66D of the Telecommunications Law — established by the previous administration — and it has primarily been used to go after Facebook posts by activists, some funny, some critical.

And there's much worse. Wai Wai freely admits that Aung San Suu Kyi was her hero. But now, like many of the women in this book and other people all over Myanmar and indeed the wider world, she is struggling — and as a Rohingya woman, that is hardly surprising.

"To be honest, when I was young, she was my role model, my hero. Because I've known about her since I was four or five. My father, he was a politician, and he had a picture of her he hid while she was under house arrest because he would have gotten into trouble for having it. And he explained how great she is you know, how dedicated. So she was my inspiration," says Wai Wai.

"But honestly, after the 2012 violence to today, I have my doubt."

The doubt has only grown as Wai Wai Nu has watched Suu Kyi's response to the latest crisis and the mass exodus of the Rohingya.

"At the beginning, I was surprised and disappointed. But now there's not time to be disappointed. We just need to fix it," says Wai Wai Nu fiercely.

She adds that she doesn't really want to use the word disappointed, because people in Myanmar almost expected too much of Suu Kyi.

"I think our society expected a lot, in terms of her being a hero for democracy and a Nobel laureate. We were expecting what she has promised to the people. But we did not realize that human beings can change. We were only promised by her words, not her actions," she says.

"She has never had power before. The fact that our society — people like me — had a lot of expectations and worshipped her as a hero — that was our overestimation. At the same time, it's not her fault. She has said she is a politician now, she has to behave as a politician."

On the other hand, Wai Wai Nu is far from absolving the Lady for her part in what is happening.

"We expect her — as a politician who respects and promotes human rights — to stand against injustice and stand for the weak. That's what I am expecting. She is a politician and can be a politician, but a politician who upholds the universality of human rights.

"This is a major suffering for her people, for her society, including the Rohingya — and for other minorities, who have been suffering side-by-side for many decades. In terms of human rights violations by the authorities, she understands it and she has to be the one who brings this onto the agenda and stands for justice."

Many people — outside Myanmar at least — agree with Wai Wai Nu, and say Aung San Suu Kyi should at least condemn the violence if she cannot stop it.

Others say that outside observers don't understand the delicate tightrope Suu Kyi must walk, carefully avoiding provoking the still powerful Burmese army at all times to avoid another coup. But others, including Wai Wai Nu (who I can't imagine being silenced by anyone), argue that that is no excuse for her silence.

"She doesn't have control over everything, but at the same time she has the responsibility to say things as they are, even if she doesn't have control," says Wai Wai Nu. "She may not have power but she has a moral obligation as de facto leader."

The latest round of violence began after a small group of Rohingya men attacked around thirty police and army posts in Rakhine State in August 2017, killing twelve officers (according to the government).

The military response was brutal; while the generals claim they have targeted militants, thousands of Rohingya civilians began fleeing almost immediately, bringing with them reports of burned villages, indiscriminate violence and mass rape. Satellite images have confirmed many villages have been wiped from the map.

But despite this, many people in Myanmar back the army's campaign against what they see as dangerous illegal immigrants (or at the very least say that reports of the violence are exaggerated), and this is another factor in Suu Kyi's silence.

There have been demonstrations in support of the army in Yangon, editorials in the newspapers, and even cartoons by former democracy campaigners depicting the Rohingya as crocodiles, biting their neighbours then crying crocodile tears about the repercussions.

A British friend in Yangon tells me she has not spoken to a single Burmese person who is against the violence — although Wai Wai Nu is not convinced.

"I don't think a lot of people support it but a lot are staying silent, and that's the problem. So those people encourage it because they have fear, but maybe also some prejudice," she says.

As such, when Suu Kyi blamed the reports on "fake news", she was playing to her audience. But not letting UN observers or even, for a period, aid into the region suggests that her position is more than just a people-pleasing tactic.

It's particularly harrowing when you hear the reports of what is happening in Rakhine; brutal stories of babies thrown into fires, entire families ripped apart, children left without family. The stories — which are consistent across thousands of testimonies — come mainly from the Rohingya who have made it across the border to Bangladesh. The refugee camp where around 900,000 Rohingya are now living has become the largest in the world.

Wai Wai says she is haunted by thoughts of the Rohingya, and, indeed, other IDPs, living in camps, comparing their imprisonment to her own.

"I think it's a much, much worse situation than I was in — I was able to get enough food, proper shelter, sleep, a bit of healthcare. But the IDPs, they don't have food, shelter, healthcare. In some they only get one meal, or they are not registered, and get nothing," she says.

"Worse, when I was in prison I was at least secure. The IDPs can be tortured at any time, beaten, killed."

But no matter how bad it gets, and no matter how hard the battle is, I don't think Wai Wai Nu will give up.

"If you say Rohingya in Myanmar you get ignorance, discrimination, or no respect," she says sadly.

"But I am so proud to be Rohingya because I know who I am and I know I, and all Rohingya, belong to this country. We have birth rights, equal rights in this country, and I don't care how you take our rights, prosecute us, discriminate. I am just as proud to be Rohingya, and I just want to be Burmese here, in my country — and no one, no government, or group, should be able to deny another person's fundamental rights."

She has so many causes — not just the current, most pressing plight of the Rohingya — and so many huge, huge battles ahead of her. I ask her why she feels she has to do what she does.

"I want to be able to hope," she says. "I want this country not to discriminate on ethnicity, religion or gender. I'm just really fed up of discrimination. So to be able to survive, I have to see less of it. Being a woman, a minority, young — I'm fed up."

Perhaps this feeling of being fed up is why, when I ask her what she is proudest of, she struggles for an answer.

"I mean … there are amazing moments," she says, eventually. "Like when I met President Obama and I was listening to his speech — and it was about me! And I was like: 'Oh! It's me!' Or when I win awards and people talk about me."

But she says one of the most astonishing and heartwarming moments in her life was when she once asked her students who their inspiration was.

"They said, oh, we want to be like you!" she laughs. "So I realized oh, they are inspired by me – so that really made me motivated and I don't realize how things are difficult or hard because I realize that what I am doing is valuable, at least for some people."

That's the flipside of how fed up Wai Wai Nu is: how she has used that feeling to motivate her to help others to believe that they don't all have to stay fed up, that things in Myanmar can change.

If this does happen, it will be down in no small part to the incredibly passionate figure you're reading about now, although — like many of the women in this book — she is probably too humble to admit it.

And based on this, I think it's fair to conclude that while calling her a princess is silly, calling her a hero certainly is not.

CHAPTER NINE

The Farmer: Mar Mar Swe

CYCLONE NARGIS — a deadly storm whose clouds have gathered ominously at various points in this book — was a tragic episode in Myanmar's recent history.

After years of man-made misery and destruction at the hands of the generals, the natural world took its turn in the early hours of 2 May 2008. A huge tropical storm tore into the south of the country, leaving devastation in its wake.

According to official figures, 84,500 people were killed in the high winds, rains and floods, the three-metre-high storm surge, and the resulting destruction of villages, bridges and roads, mainly in the coastal Ayeyarwady Delta region.

A further 53,800 were reported missing, later presumed dead, possibly swept out to sea in the storm.

In reality, probably many more were hit. The UN has estimated that up to 2.4 million people were affected by Nargis, Myanmar's worst ever natural disaster. Millions were left homeless.

While Yangon also suffered, it was in the Ayeyarwady region that the storm really wreaked havoc. Many people there live simple lives as subsistence farmers or fishermen, and Nargis destroyed up to 95 per cent of buildings in some areas, as well as decimating crops and livelihoods.

The tragedy was exacerbated when the ruling military junta initially forbade international aid from coming into the country, a ban that was overturned after global outcry.

But figures like this can be hard to quantify. For Mar Mar Swe, a female farmer living close to Bogale in the delta region, the horror was much closer to home.

She had already had a rough few years. Her husband had died after many years of illness, leaving her alone with their baby son and other children, and badly in debt. Then came Nargis.

"I had been struggling, but then Nargis hit, and it destroyed my properties and my houses," she says. "It was a nightmare time for me. I suffered so much."

Things hadn't always been so bad for Mar Mar Swe. When she and her husband married, they received around eight acres of land from their families in their home village of Kyee Chaung. Like around 70 per cent of Myanmar's population, they lived rurally, supporting themselves. For a while, they were happy, working their land and looking after their kids.

Then Mar Mar Swe's husband began to get sick. He was ill for a long time, and in Myanmar, illness is expensive. Mar Mar Swe had to borrow a lot of money from the village moneylender for his treatment and medication.

"I worried all the time," she says, twisting her hands in her lap as she speaks to me via a translator in a roadside restaurant in her nearest large-ish town, Bogale. Paying the loan back was an almost impossible dream — and the hefty 10 per cent monthly interest payments were crippling.

Then things worsened. Her husband died in 2003, and she was forced to sell several acres of their farmland.

"We had many debts, so I had to sell the land of the farm — according to our beliefs, when people die, in order to have a good life in their next life they cannot have debts. So I had to pay our debts," says Mar Mar Swe.

She sold five acres of their land. Although the sale helped in the short-term, she and her family then spent the next five years living hand-to-mouth, forced into spiralling debt with unscrupulous moneylenders in order to survive, to plant paddy in her remaining fields, and grow seasonal vegetables. Each year, as well as the moneylender, she had to take out loans on her remaining three acres to be able to afford to plant anything.

"I struggled for around six years," she remembers. Mar Mar Swe has been garrulous and friendly as we talk, but she is clearly reluctant to go back to the difficult years. She sums them up shortly. "A hard time," she says.

A hard time at the end of which was Nargis — but also, after that, hope. And I'm meeting Mar Mar Swe because of that hope; because, in the face of such trying times, she didn't give up. Instead, the forty-three-year-old became one of a band of female farmers in Myanmar who are redefining what it's like to lead your family out of difficult circumstances.

For Mar Mar Swe, the first step was hearing about and getting in touch with a local microfinance firm. The Pact Global Microfinance Project, funded by the UN's LIFT (Livelihoods and Food Security Trust Fund) project, gave her a way out, in the same way that microfinance has for many people living on the edge all over the world.

Microfinance lenders do what they say on the tin: provide small loans to individuals, at reasonable repayment and interest rates. Their business is a world away from the greedy local moneylenders of Mar Mar Swe's past.

Her first loan was for 70,000 kyat (around US$50). She used it to buy some ducklings and start a duckling farm, an idea she got from one of her neighbours. Each duckling cost just 650 kyat (less than US$0.50). But their food and shelter was expensive, and it was a risk.

It paid off: four months after buying the ducklings, they began to lay eggs. With the steady income and the lower interest rate of 2.5 per cent for the repayments, Mar Mar Swe began to clear her debts. Her duck farm grew, and the pressures began to ease.

After two years, ducks stop laying, and are sold for meat. Mar Mar Swe began to diversify. She still has the duck farm, but she also now has a three-acre paddy farm, a betel (a mild stimulant chewed by many in Myanmar) plantation, a vegetable garden and a fish farm.

The fish farm is a recent success, and testament to Mar Mar Swe's growing confidence as a businesswoman.

"The initial cost is high — each fish trap costs around 7,000 kyat

(US$5). But my brother suggested it would be worthwhile to invest so I took a 500,000 kyat loan (US$365) and started buying the traps," says Mar Mar Swe.

"It is going well — the earnings from the business are quite good. Whenever I go to market to sell the fish, I get around 20,000–30,000 kyat (up to US$20, a sizeable sum in this low-income country). I sell them every four or five days, and it can be quite lucrative."

In fact, with two of her older sons now also working in Yangon (her two youngest children, a son of fourteen and a daughter of nine, still live with her in the delta), she describes her situation now as "getting prosperous". She has no worries about paying back any of her loans, and her darkest hours feel a long way away.

And while she is open to taking suggestions from others, she feels the moment that she realized she was the only person who could change her own life was the moment she really pulled herself and her family out of those dark hours. That's why she is prepared to take the risks she has, from the ducklings onwards.

"All of the important decisions are made by me," she says. "With the loan, I like the feeling that I can do what I like without taking help from the outside. This is helpful for my family."

I ask her if this is important, this idea of doing things herself.

"Yes, of course," she replies, laughing. "I'm not going to sacrifice myself for the leadership of men. I know it is up to me."

Mar Mar Swe has since remarried — she met her husband in 2008, just after her duckling business got going, and her two youngest children are with him. And while she is happy to have his support, she is equally happy that he goes out to work in construction in Yangon (about a four-hour drive away) and leaves the farm to her to run.

"It was my decision for him to do that, and my decision to start the fish trapping business recently," she says.

She now manages the farm with her nephews, who share the yield. She is the manager and does the ploughing and organizing of the paddy, as well as looking after the overall strategy for their brood of seventy ducks and thirty fish traps. Her nephews do the harvesting.

Her day begins at 5.30 a.m.

"I prepare the food for the family— I don't need to go to the market for this because we have the garden and the fish traps and the ducklings, so I only need to cook," she says.

"At around 7 a.m., I go to the duck farms, collect the eggs and release the ducks into the streams and fields, and then I collect vegetables. This takes me three or four hours."

She has a little free time before noon, and a little after, but then she has to prepare the vegetables and eggs for sale in Bogale market the next day. After that, she needs to cook again for the family, collect more eggs, feed the ducks, and do more work in the garden.

Every three days or so, she leaves her house at 4 a.m. by boat to take her wares to market, and finishes selling there by about 10 a.m. It's hot, dusty and intense — but Mar Mar Swe enjoys the hustle and bustle, and likes to keep busy.

"That's my routine," she smiles. And there are high points. For example, Mar Mar Swe has built up a pretty unique relationship with her ducks. When she quacks, they follow her. She laughs a lot when I ask her about this, obviously amused by my interest in such a mundane part of her life.

"They don't understand what I am saying, but they understand sounds, and I can call them back to me by making that sound," she says.

It's great to watch, and she isn't exaggerating: the ducklings follow her exactly as they would follow their Mother Duck. But this Mother Duck means business, and she's doing it in a man's world.

"Sometimes it is difficult for me, for women to deal with other men in business," she admits.

"For example, when we sell the paddy, the men sometimes pretend they don't understand my calculations, and try to cheat me," she says.

I doubt this happens for long though. There's a steely backbone of determination in Mar Mar Swe that suggests she wouldn't be cheated twice. Under her *thanaka*, a paste worn by many Burmese women as part sun-protection, part decoration, I don't doubt that she is as tough as any of the men who try to cheat her. She is also thirsty for knowledge, asking me first about where I'm from, then about farming in the U.K., then about the food in Yangon — perhaps with an eye for further business expansion.

In fact, she's so worldly that I'm shocked, when we later drive through town in a UN car, that she feels carsick. She never travels in cars; in the delta, most travel is done by boat, where she is much more comfortable.

She hopes now that her story can be an inspiration for other women.

"In the past, the men did the business, and the women were only for housework. But these days, men and women both earn together and the role of the man and woman can be the same in business. This is obviously a good thing," she says.

She thinks her country is only going to change more and more as people see the potential of women like her.

"Most families in Myanmar are led by the husband, but there are a few cases like me, where the woman does not rely on her husband. So now we are coming forward and making important decisions," she says.

And her next step is to start trading the products of the delta in the dry zone of the country. She wants to take her fish and fish paste, key delta products, and trade them for the garments and clothes made in the drier zones of the middle of the country.

"And I want to do it by myself," she says, grinning once again. "The trading, the travelling, the return journeys. Maybe at that time I will ask my husband to manage my farm! Or sometimes I will send him to trade. That's my future plan."

I wouldn't put it past her.

CHAPTER TEN

The Pop Star: Ah Moon

BURMESE POP star Ah Moon is reading out her social media messages as we sit in the Yangon traffic.

"Bitch, slut, get out of the country," she says, scrolling down. "And it's just because I'm wearing what I want. But when people call me things because of what I'm wearing, or showing skin, I think they need to see that I'm a human, a woman, and showing your body as a woman, and showing your abilities, and raising your voice — there's nothing wrong with that."

Her jaw juts defiantly, and we pull away from the traffic in her car.

"I'm in a situation where I push boundaries every day," she says. "It's not because I'm not respectful to people, it's because I want to show people from Myanmar that just because you are from this country, you don't need to box yourself in. You can be out of the box, you can look at the outside world, and I think catching up is not a wrong thing."

Ah Moon, twenty-five, is one of Myanmar's leading pop stars. Think of her as the Beyoncé of Destiny's Child, or the Harry Styles of One Direction — her career started in a talent show, then a girl band (one of Myanmar's first), and she has emerged from that as her own woman, with a string of hits under her belt, a film, and more than a million followers on Facebook.

Apart from that you can't really think of her like Harry or Beyoncé, because she's actually far more revolutionary than that.

Under the military junta, making music in Myanmar was effectively banned, and things have been very slow to change since then. While there were some brave acts out there who tried to produce original sounds, in the main, pop music was made up of Burmese copies of Western hits called copy tracks, for many years. Even then, censorship was everywhere.

When a military-backed civilian government took over from the generals in 2011, things improved, although not immediately. Ah Moon's former group — the Me N Ma Girls — remember celebrating because they were allowed to wear coloured wigs in one of their videos.

In 2012, they released "Mingalar Par" — a word used as a greeting in Myanmar, particularly to foreigners — with some pretty bold lyrics. Singing partly in Burmese and partly in English, wearing a mix of traditional clothes and Western outfits, their mission was clear: to emerge from behind the closed doors of their country and remind the world that they were the same as everyone else.

"I'm a girl from the land of Myanmar, try to sing it loud so my voice reach far. Myanmar girls, just like any other girl in the world," they sang. It's basically been a mission statement for Ah Moon ever since.

The group was formed in 2010, via a talent show in a Yangon bar. Five girls, including Ah Moon, were chosen by Australian dancer Nicole May and Burmese entrepreneur U Moe Kyaw. At first they too had to release copy songs, and were called the Tiger Girls.

"It was exciting but it was tiring — but it was so cool because we were the very first girl band," says Ah Moon. "At first people didn't even know what we were doing, so we had to make them understand what we are."

She's underplaying it a bit: the group were deliberately chosen to look different than the typical K-pop (Korean pop) stars, to wear modern outfits and perform and dance with more freedom. They may not have initially set out to change their country — and perceptions of the women within it (Ah Moon says at the time it was just her dream to be on stage, performing) — but they did.

At that time, and in many ways it is still the case today, much of the Burmese public equated women performing in bars with sex workers. Touring was also taboo, in part because of the parental-set curfews many unmarried Burmese women keep. Not so for the Tiger Girls, who soon became the rather more catchy Me N Ma Girls, solely under the management of May.

In an interview with the *New York Times* in 2012, author Heather MacLachlan — who had written *Burma's Pop Music Industry: Creators, Distributors, Censors* in 2011 — summed up the impact of the band and their catchy boy-meets-girl lyrics and pop videos. In any other culture, they would have been typical (dancing, swimming, hanging out, wearing short dresses), but in Myanmar, they were game-changing.

"I've *never* seen girls [in Myanmar] behave like that, ever," she said. So the band were fighting on two fronts: first, to get over the censorship and repression still at the heart of their new government, and second, to flip traditional gender roles completely upside down.

In 2012, the Me N Ma Girls even wrote their first overtly political song, *Come Back Home*, directed at those who had left Myanmar due to the repression and poverty of the preceding decades. It was first performed for the former U.S. Ambassador for Global Women's Issues, Melanne Verveer.

The group were spotted by LA Management, which simultaneously launched them on the global stage and led to some problems. Ah Moon was pushed to the front because of her language skills (her English is flawless, and she speaks four other languages too — Burmese, Kachin, French and Russian). This caused resentment in the band, which disintegrated over the course of the next few years.

As part of the Me N Ma Girls, Ah Moon's stage name was "Baby", à *la* The Spice Girls, Britain's era-defining girl band of the 1990s. But it is no baby I meet in 2016 (her latest album features the defiant lyrics, interspersed with Burmese: "Everybody wants to call me a crazy bitch").

She's sorry the band broke up, but considers it inevitable considering the personalities in the group.

"We were not sisters, and even with your siblings you want to fight. I had a really good time with them but the main thing which differentiated us was how badly you want this. I wanted to be an artist, a real one, and I didn't care what I had to do to achieve this," says Ah Moon.

"Sometimes the others were like, no, I don't want to do that because I'm on my period, so that became hard. I wanted to go international, and I thought we all did, but when the hard work comes, it becomes difficult."

She isn't joking about hard work. I shadow Ah Moon for a few days and I've never known a schedule like it. She drives us around Yangon, snatching a few moments here and there to eat hard-boiled eggs to keep her going. We go from a shoot at a make-up parlour to a chat show appearance, from the gym to a show, and I'm exhausted. She started the day before 7 a.m., and at 11 p.m., when she's still smiling and signing autographs in the heat of the Burmese night, I'm out.

She still has a manager in LA, and a personal assistant, but she does a lot of the behind the scenes work herself, too — for example, managing her wildly popular Facebook page.

"I like to do it," she says. "I wish I could let someone else do it, but most of the time I have to check it again, to make sure it is right. Eventually I'll have someone but right now I need to learn how things go here."

I think she's also a natural leader, who likes things to be in their natural order — in a later Whatsapp message, she laughingly tells me she has trypophobia, a fear of irregular patterns or clusters of holes or bumps. Considering the military precision of her schedule, with everything in its place, I'm not surprised.

But a female pop star who not only sings about girl power and wears what she wants, but also wants to manage her own career, in Myanmar? It's a big ask.

"I sometimes meet people and they are like, oh you're just a little girl trying to be bossy," she says. "I think it's because the world is used to the man's society. It's not just here, in developing countries; I think even in the West a girl is going to get called a bossy girl if she's in charge of everything."

She's not wrong, and it's with comments like this that she shows she is so much more than just a manufactured pop star.

"Is this just human nature, this idea that girls need to be less strong because we are girls?" she says. "I think this is what human beings have accepted, but it can change. Power doesn't depend on if you are a boy or a girl, it's how strong you want to be in your life. I think girls have been told that this is human nature throughout history — you know, man's power — and girls still have to fight to get equally paid all over the world. So we should be doing the best to have equal rights with men."

Despite comments like this, Ah Moon doesn't see herself as a feminist.

"It's because I don't really know what that word means, it has a lot of meanings and I just want to fight to get equal rights as a girl, that's all," she says. We're discussing this in her kitchen, where she is making eggs for her dancer before their run of eleven shows in five days begins later that day. She's wearing a onesie, and flip flops with stars and moons on them — as she says, just like any other girl in the world.

She adds: "When I see the word feminism, I feel lower — like, why do we need this label?"

I tell her I think she sounds a bit like Maisie Williams, the *Game of Thrones* actress who once said she too was uncomfortable with the word feminist, explaining: "You're either a normal person, or a sexist."

Ah Moon agrees immediately (and says *Game of Thrones* is next on her watch-list).

"In that way we are all feminists, we can say that, but it's the label that's difficult. It's more important to do it than to say it," she says.

In that way, Ah Moon is certainly trying to "do" feminism, and perhaps that's surprising considering her fairly traditional background. A Christian from Kachin State, in the north of the country, her father is a pastor. But she gets angry when people suggest that his job might mean he disapproves of her bold choices.

"I think my dad — and my mom — they believe in me, they trust me. They know my passion, and my dad tells me sometimes he is worried because of how people might see me, but then he said, I know what you are doing, and I know that you are just being different from people, and he said — 'I get it'," says Ah Moon, whose full Kachin name is Lung Sitt Ja Moon.

He doesn't like the comments she gets, but he has learned to handle it.

"He's a protective dad too. But we're cool, and he's so cool," she adds.

The family's relationship is obviously close: they moved to Yangon when Ah Moon was nine, and she still lives in the same apartment complex as them.

"It helps me not forget where I'm from," she says simply. And considering her success, the apartment is relatively simple. It isn't small, but it isn't huge, and it feels much like any other Burmese apartment (with some typical pop star, or perhaps just young woman, touches — piles and piles of shoes in the doorway, a mad kitten roaming the halls, guitars and keyboards strewn around, and a glittering picture of a tiger in the entrance).

She says her family, who are all musical inside church and outside it, are proud of her.

"My dad is the one who went to the market when I was born and got a tape player and put it beside me. I was the first daughter, and he played music and prayed for me — be a musician," she remembers. "The first time I performed with a live band is when I as four years old. And my Mum said I was like — what do you call it? Side eye! – looking at the guy when he did the wrong beat. But I loved it."

And she says their faith, and her faith, helps her get through the challenges of pushing boundaries in the way she does.

"They are so positive, and they have given me so much love since I was born, and that's why I sometimes think I can be overly confident. But for an artist who is criticized every day, you have to be overly confident," she says.

Perhaps to help maintain that confidence, she also confesses that she talks to herself in the mirror when she's feeling stressed. At the same time, she feels she can also turn to God — and her God is one who does not judge others — when she needs him.

"I grew up with Christianity, church, and it's important to me. But I don't want to be a Christian who points at others, oh, you don't go to church or whatever. Just be a good Christian, be good to people. And I believe in God, whom we can't really see or express, but we can connect to. And every day I wake up and connect to him — or her, haha," she says.

And if it all sounds too cosy and comfortable a background to produce an artist, Ah Moon points out that it has not all been plain sailing. She writes her arguments, fights and experiences into her music, she says — brandishing her phone at me to show me the poems and lyrics she is working on at the moment — and then proceeds to tell me a really harrowing story about an ex-boyfriend when I ask her about other relationships outside her family.

"Well, I'm kind of scared of relationships since I broke up with my boyfriend and he kidnapped me," she says.

Wait a second, I reply. What?

"Yeah, I dated a psychopath, by the way," she says, lightly.

"Because I said goodbye, he locked me up in his flat. He told me to come and get my stuff, then he locked me in. This was in 2013, and it was crazy. Luckily I found the key in the end — and he was just a bad person — but I need to put the time and energy into myself at the moment."

It's quite a shocking tale, and one which has only re-enforced her bid for independence, but she breezes over it into talking about her plans to have a big family in the future (she has three brothers). She is in a new relationship nowadays, but doesn't talk about it much in public, feeling that some parts of her life should stay private. It's a big step and suggests to me that things are quite serious: Ah Moon is dedicated to sharing things with her fans (she calls them her "stars") and spent a recent period of fairly serious illness writing a book for girls full of advice about dealing with life in a man's world, and vlogging her low moments.

Her relationship with her fans, therefore, is touching and honest, and whenever we spent time together, it was sweet to watch her interact with them. That's what makes it even harder, she says, when she feels like she has betrayed them because of something she has to do to fit in.

For example, she was recently involved in giving the prize in a competition for a beer brand that was broadcast live on Facebook. It was a lucky dip, and the prize was a substantial amount of cash. Before she went on air, both the Burmese and the Western representatives of the beer company told her to cover up.

"I was disgusted. I mean, maybe in my culture, but for the foreigner? They know better," she spits. It got worse. She was told that if she picked a woman's name, that wasn't the image the brand wanted, and she should throw it back into the bucket. She objected, but before she had time to make a scene, the competition went live.

She picked a name. It was a woman's name. The host took it, and then tossed it aside, saying that someone had forgotten to write a name. Stuck, Ah Moon picked again. This time it was a man's name, and he won the money.

"It was just … I mean, we have so far to go," she says to me over lunch a few days later (we go to a Kachin restaurant near her house, and she is thrilled that I think it is the most delicious food I've tried in Myanmar, fresh and spicy). I try to reassure her that at least she is doing something, fighting for women's rights with every short skirt she wears or vaguely racy lyric she writes.

That in itself sometimes still gets her in trouble with the censorship board, which is by no means dormant under the new government led by Aung San Suu Kyi, despite The Lady's international reputation as an icon of free speech.

"In one of my [recent] music videos, they cut it off because we — my friends and I — were wearing short skirts or shorts, and we were in front of Sule Pagoda," she says, referring to an iconic landmark in central Yangon. "I just want the world to hear from us, hear from our unique culture and style, but people here, and especially the censorship board, think that when we mix with Western culture we are ruining our own culture. That's something I can't agree with," she says.

She's pleased to see other women increasingly wearing what they want in Yangon, from shorts to tank tops. Or indeed the traditional *longyi*, but she still thinks there's a double standard.

"When they see me up on stage they say things, and it's all bullshit, because you see people now wearing what they want in Yangon, kids on a night out, people clubbing. It's changing. But then I get all the social media stuff and blah blah and the censorship board. I didn't see any young people on that board, they're just sitting there censoring the youth's creativity," says Ah Moon.

Her work isn't just censored for what she wears, either. In a similar vein, her attempts to blend Burmese traditional music and pop are also blocked.

"We are censored all the time. One of my songs was cut off the album because I used the words "*Sin eh wa*", these catchy lyrics and rhythms from a traditional song. And my song is about young love and being sexy, and I just wanted to use these traditional rhythms. But they said no, and it is frustrating. I just want people in the world to hear it and be like, oh what is that, and learn," she says. "I hope — it might take ten years — but I hope in the future we can do what we want to do artistically."

You get the sense that for Ah Moon — and indeed, probably for many of her fans and her generation — change cannot come quickly enough. Despite the setbacks, she's still happy to see Aung San Suu Kyi effectively at the head of her country, not least because she's a woman; but she says there is so much still to do.

"It's not all fine, it's not all fine here in Burma," she says. "If it was all fine, then the [political] prisoners in Insein Jail could come out. We have to wait, although I do hope she and her party can lead the country to a better level. We've been left behind for many, many years. It's just the start yet, and I hope it can change fast enough."

In the meantime, she's determined to try and change things in her own way — even if sometimes it is hard.

"It gets me sometimes because when you're trying to follow your dreams, and make something internationally, and change things, and people here say that you're wrong and because you're born here, you can't do this," she says. "But I find my own truth and I'm chasing my dreams — I wanted to be a singer, a songwriter, a dancer, and I want people to have fun with what I make. So I'm happy with that."

Now, she says, when she checks her social media feeds and she sees the familiar bitch, slut, comments, she is, strangely, almost reassured. At least she's having an impact.

"I'm like, ah, I can start my day now. I take it as noise — and I keep going," she says. And she says she will keep on going to make sure that the message she and her band mates sang about back in 2012 — that Myanmar girls are just like any other girls — hits home in the rest of the world.

As she explains this to me, her voice cracks a little and I can see tears shining in her eyes.

"I'm trying to come out into the world, and I've been pulled back, and I want them to know about my struggle here," she says, wiping at her eyes and shrugging a little with embarrassment at her own emotion.

"I will not give up and I'll keep pushing and moving. These girls in the developed world who think in a different way to girls in Burma, they are very lucky that they can have their freedom to do what they want in their lives. I just want them to know about me, us, my music and my art, and that we are all the same."

CHAPTER ELEVEN

The Politician: Htin Htin Htay

HTIN HTIN Htay is speaking in a low, urgent voice. The late afternoon sun is creeping around the roof of her wooden house, throwing shadows on the decked balcony where we are speaking. Confused cockerels are crowing below us.

She is telling me her childhood memories.

"In this village here, at midnight, the government soldiers came to force us to relocate to other places," she says.

"I remember. I was eight years old. We had to move before 10 a.m. They said that if anyone remained in the village they would be killed. In fact, they said we would be like ash, flown away into the air, finished."

Terrified by the threat, Htin Htin's family fled as instructed, taking very little other than what they had with them at that moment. A few days later, they went back to see what food or personal items they could collect.

"We went to check the village. I saw a lot of dead bodies, being put under the bridge. So I said to my mum, what is that? And she told me not to look, it is too scary. But I saw a woman praying to the army not to arrest her husband, so they cut off her hands and shot the husband. I saw that," she says.

It's a long time ago — Htin Htin Htay is now thirty-four years old — but she still remembers what she saw, and what, as a child, she shouldn't ever have had to see, back in the 1980s and early 1990s in military-run southern Myanmar.

She goes on: "And then a doctor who had come to cure diseases, they asked him about his background with the rebel group. He did not answer, so they cut off his tongue and tortured him, and he died. The villagers could hear him yell and shout because of the pain, but nobody dared help him. I saw that kind of thing when I was eight years old. That is my background, growing up in a black area."

When talking about Myanmar's conflict-hit areas, a black area means a place held by insurgents or ethnic armies (white is government-controlled, and brown contested). For Htin Htin Htay, that was her home, the village of Oattu in Tanintharyi region, the south of the country — about an hour's motorbike ride from the nearest big city, Dawei.

The black areas are notorious, and Myanmar's state army, the Tatmadaw, had (and in some cases still has) a brutal policy for the civilians remaining within them. The civilians are forcibly relocated — with the emphasis on force — and there have also been reports of enforced labour, looting, rape and summary executions conducted by soldiers acting with impunity.

For example, one study conducted by the International Human Rights Clinic at Harvard University, which involved testimony from soldiers on the ground after a Tatmadaw offensive in Karen state in 2005–08, reported soldiers being told to treat all civilians as potential rebels and combatants, and to act accordingly (for more on the Karen conflict, see Chapter 7).

There is no reason to believe that their policy was any different in Htin Htin Htay's area.

In her area, she says the rebels were part of the All Burma Students' Democratic Front (ABSDF). Burmese student activists were at the forefront of protests against the junta in 1988. Many fled after the government crackdown on protesters, and formed protest groups in the jungles and on the borders of the country. The ABSDF went further than most, forming an armed wing to advance their cause of freedom for Myanmar soon after the protests.

The group was on the U.S. terror list until 2010, but at the same time some of its leaders were granted asylum. The group fought alongside other ethnic armies, and agreed a ceasefire with the government in 2013.

Before this, Htin Htin Htay and other civilians were simply caught in the crossfire, and often became the victims of a ruthless state military.

"The government soldiers had come to my house before," she remembers. "They were looking for money or gold and didn't see anything, so they pulled my father out of the door. He was paralysed with tuberculosis. He was not a heavy person, he was sick, so they just left him out there in the rain."

After her family fled their village back in 1990, things did not improve. Although they had been saving money for the potential escape, aware that the worst might happen, they had to spend it quickly on essentials like a bamboo roof for their flimsy shelter a few miles down the road. They spent around eighteen months effectively camped there. Other friends fled to Thailand as refugees.

"We had nothing," says Htin Htin Htay. Eventually, her family were allowed to return to their garden to collect vegetables for their food (the army troop leader had been staying in their house). After a year or so of doing that, they came back "little by little", as she puts it. They had to leave the village by 4 p.m. every day and have a full body-check as they left, to see if they were smuggling letters or anything else. They were also checked at the new temporary village by the road. There were checkpoints, and many villagers were forced into work for the army. Htin Htin Htay's father died when they returned from the forced relocation camp after eighteen months of struggle.

As some of the other chapters of this book have shown, tragically, there is nothing unique about Htin Htin Htay's story. In fact, Tanintharyi is considered one of the calmer regions of Myanmar, and fighting there was much rarer than in other regions — some of which are still in conflict today.

However, this relatively calm region did not escape the violence altogether, and my translator backs up Htin Htin Htay's memories, telling me that the jungle villages in the area were famously some of the hardest hit by fighting in the local area in the last thirty years. The violence left a long shadow.

"After around ten years, it became stable, but until now, people have not dared come back to this village," says Htin Htin Htay.

But for this remarkable woman, the violence had the opposite effect.

I'm here to see her because she is one of only a tiny handful of women holding vitally important roles in local politics in Myanmar — and her childhood directly inspired her political contribution.

Being a woman on Myanmar's political scene is complicated (as it still is in more developed countries too, including the United States and the United Kingdom). While Aung San Suu Kyi is a shining example right at the top of Burmese politics, the picture gets bleaker the further down the chain of power you go. For example, the percentage of female MPs in parliament doubled at the landmark 2015 elections, but they still only represent 13 per cent of the elected seats. When the military representatives are taken into account (the military still holds 25 per cent of the seats across Myanmar's two houses of government), this goes down to 9.7 per cent.

Right at the coalface of local politics and administration are the local village tract administrators, vital figures in communities across Myanmar who oversee everything from road-building to divorce. There are 16,785 village tract administrators. Just sixty-eight of them — or 0.4 per cent — are women. And Htin Htin Htay is one of them.

I ask her whether what she saw as a child motivated her to make a difference, and she speaks passionately in the local Tavoyan dialect. My translator — a pretty cool woman herself, head of the local Tavoy Women's Association in Dawei who brought me to the village on the back of her motorbike — says Htin Htin Htay is struggling to control her emotions, and we wait.

Then she continues.

"Since I was a little girl, I saw the situation here. I saw one day the forced labour for the military. The villagers were collecting the paddy for the troops, not for themselves. Then some old ladies were being slow and so the former village administrator, he beat them, and he kicked them, shouting: 'You are slow, make it faster!'" she says.

"So because the soldiers can kill us, can shoot us, that is what I have seen, and I thought, why? Why do people kill, why can't we respond? So this situation remains in my body, in my blood, in my heart, and that is why I have to do this — this is what encouraged me to work as a leader."

Before she took on the job as a village tract administrator (VTA), Htin Htin Htay trained as a lawyer, and she says the corruption and injustice she saw as a child also motivated her to take on this role.

"In my community, whenever there is a case, we have to pay money to the police, the lawyer, the judge. We don't call it paying — it's like a bribe — so we have to pay money from the beginning, so until recently, the winner is just always the one who has the most money," she says. "So I wanted to help people."

She became a lawyer by studying at night through distance learning, a sign of the determination which also saw her elected as a VTA.

"My parents work in the garden and our plantation, so I helped them. Then regular education is too expensive for me so I studied by distance education, by letter, then three months together with the class, then an exam," she explains.

Her legal career is now on hold while she juggles the responsibilities of being a VTA. She was elected in March 2016, after the previous candidate was barred from election because he had once been in prison. You can tell Htin Htin Htay believes that this mix-up was more political than official — if he had had the right letter, he might still have been able to stand (being in prison is hardly a barrier to elected office in Myanmar, where scores of those now in power — including Aung San Suu Kyi — have been incarcerated in some form or another).

He represented Aung San Suu Kyi's party, the National League for Democracy (NLD), and so does Htin Htin Htay; she stepped up on his recommendation to prevent the old military-backed political party, the Union Solidarity and Development Party (USDP), from taking the village.

"The party picked me because I was the most qualified," says Htin Htin Htay, who has experience campaigning with the NLD and with other community campaigns. She also knew the chief minister in the division and other VTAs.

But her choice was still surprising to many, as was her election, even though she won a clear majority of the fifty-one votes from local household leaders who turned up on election day.

"For the village it was very strange to pick a woman," she admits. "It was almost unbelievable in fact, because no women have led the community or the village before. But for me, it is not so strange, because according to the law, anyone can be a VTA. There is no discrimination between men and women, and some villages have female VTAs already. So for me it is fine."

However, she does say she has experienced some people who believe she is not fit for the job because of her gender — people who have pointed out that the curfews many Burmese women live by would make it difficult for her to do things at night, for example. Htin Htin Htay is single, and lives with her mother.

"The opposition said, if you select a woman, how can she go out at night, what if she has to go somewhere at midnight? In the past, with the rebel groups, they would come and ask for taxation from the village. So the village leader has to handle this, and they were saying how can she handle this? How can a woman handle that, if they come at midnight, you know?"

But it hasn't been a problem.

"I have not had any issues like that, but I don't care if I do — I am not afraid since the beginning. Whether they come or not, I can handle it. I believe that I am a leader," says Htin Htin Htay. And her fearless attitude has won round some of the doubters.

"I don't think it is hard for the men to take my rule. Before I was elected we already had an agreement that if I have to go out at midnight or whatever, other committee members who are men have offered that they will go out and do, or we can go together. So it is not harder for me," she says.

The job certainly keeps her busy, though. Her mobile rings three or four times while we talk, and she runs me through her duties.

"For example, at the school there is a waterway — so I have to go and check, are the students able to access water regularly or not? So we have to open our eyes and listen to the community. We have four meetings a month, and I also go to meetings with the chief minister and at the township level," she says.

"Also, people write to me as the VTA, because they think all the jobs have to be taken by the VTA, but I delegate with the group, with the household leaders."

Her first job on election was fixing the roads that led to the village.

"There was a new monastery so we celebrated it with an opening ceremony, and other villages came and attended this, so I had to lead the road work quickly. Later, we will repair all the roads in the village," she says.

Money comes from the government and local taxation for these endeavours. For Htin Htin Htay's remuneration, the position is not paid, as such — there's a stipend of 70,000 kyat a month (around US$50), and another stationery stipend of around 50,000 kyat (US$35). It's for things like printing newsletters, and paying for travel and other materials. Htin Htin Htay says there is very little left for her at the end of the month.

But she still loves the work. We meet at a house near her own in the village, surrounded by other women who are meeting to talk about their own challenges jointly with Htin Htin Htay and the Tavoy Women's Association.

She sees it as her role particularly to help other women, something she traces back to her main inspiration in life: her mum.

"After my dad passed away, my mum was good at saving money and bought the garden. Thieves can take gold and money, but not the garden. With our garden, we had food, so we did not lose face or get treated as poor people, because of my mum. She is a really great woman — really clever," says Htin Htin Htay.

But despite the example from her mum, she realized at an early age that most women did not experience this kind of freedom.

"When I was little I thought it was important to be a woman leader in the community or government, because I saw how they discriminated against women always. Even now, I am a leader, and I went to attend a meeting. I like to sit at the front and listen, and I was told that women don't sit here, they sit at the back. This is [the policy of] an official government department — and I don't like this," she says.

She puts discrimination like this down to social norms and traditional practice, but hopes it can change.

"Men are even leaders in the family — for the boy, they leave curries before the women eat. But for me, I was growing up with a widowed woman, and my mum could lead our family of six. She is my role model — because she did it, she led our family, I can do it. That is why women can do it."

And Htin Htin is now going even further than her trailblazing mother — she isn't just trying to live like a man in a man's world (which many feminists in the Western world are forced to do to get ahead). Instead, she is reclaiming her power for women — she sees no reason to fit into male patterns of strength in order to be a strong leader for her community.

"Traditionally, the VTA has to speak louder, be rigid, be tough. But I have always said since the beginning, don't keep me in the box like that. I will stay as my own person. Many people say the VTA should speak louder, show power, be rich — but I am gentle, that is my style," she says.

She hopes her example can inspire other girls and women in the village. But first, she needs to get to work helping them realize their potential.

"First of all, in the summer many of the families withdraw their students from school because they are doing the rubber plantation. And the girls, they get married and they don't finish their education or go to further education. So I want to stop this, and help them get education," she says.

Htin Htin Htay is modest, saying she will hand over power soon if there are better candidates, but I hope — and so do the women I speak to in her village — that she realizes how much of a positive force she is in her area and stays in her role.

"I never pray for myself. I always pray for other people. My interest is giving education to other people, so I want to do more of this," she says.

And she's a long way from finished yet, whether or not she thinks that better candidates could be waiting in the wings. What's next, I ask?

"I have so many things to do in this area!" she cries, before listing everything from improving education for all to sorting out those potholed roads, once-and-for-all. The list is pretty long. Perhaps she'll be in the job longer than she thinks.

CHAPTER TWELVE

The Archer: Aung Ngeain

MOST PEOPLE have heard of Myanmar's ghost-like capital city, Naypyidaw.

Unveiled by the military junta back in 2005, and built from scratch for reportedly billions of dollars, the capital has been a soulless white elephant in the middle of the country ever since. It even has its very own white elephants (in Myanmar they are seen as lucky), living in cages at the base of the bizarre, near full-size replica of Shwedagon Pagoda on the edge of the town.

What it doesn't have, famously, is people. Instead, it has deserted twenty-lane highways, Vegas-style hotels without any guests, and golf courses frequented only infrequently by top generals and politicians. It also draws curious film crews from across the globe — the BBC's *Top Gear* team played football and even held a drag race on its empty boulevards on their visit.

The city was built by the regime at speed for reasons that are still vague. Rumours range from the junta's paranoia over the ease of invading Yangon to astrological predictions regarding the auspiciousness of Naypyidaw's location. Whatever the thinking, it happened quickly: civil servants were reportedly ordered to relocate there within 48 hours, although many chose to stay in Yangon and still commute on a weekly basis, via a 5-hour bus trip.

But in the new semi-democratic era, things are changing a little. Some of the politicians and civil servants of the new administration have made their homes here. Other people who live in the surrounding villages come into the city for work. And others have been drawn to its infrastructure and facilities, which are unequalled anywhere else in the country.

That's what brought Aung Ngeain, 31, here. She's a fantastically successful Burmese archer, probably the most successful ever, with twenty-seven gold medals from international competitions.

Nowadays, she works as an archery trainer, trying to find — well, trying to find the next Aung Ngeain, amid Naypyidaw's bright lights and shiny targets.

It's a long way, literally and metaphorically, from where it all started for her.

She grew up in a town in Chin state called Mindat, where her father was a teacher and her mother made cloth. She describes their background as "poor" in a state which, as we have already seen in Chapter 1, is poor enough in itself.

"Everything was remote in Chin state then. We had never seen a telephone. I didn't think phones existed before I went to Yangon," says Aung Ngeain.

"There was a road, but it was not good enough to travel on. There was no development, no technology. But as a child I thought it was normal. Though now when I look back on my childhood, I think it was very difficult."

Aung Ngeain's fairy godmother came in the unlikely shape of a group of archery trainers, who visited her town when she was aged seventeen on the hunt for new talent to represent Myanmar.

Aung Ngeain had never picked up a bow, or even thought about archery. She liked volleyball. She wasn't even going to go to the try-outs; her friend persuaded her.

"She said, 'Come with me together. If you don't come with me, I won't go.' Her favourite sport was archery, and she really wanted to become a famous archer," says Aung Ngeain.

But after the three-week course, when the kids started off with toy bows and arrows and saw their skills progressively tested, her friend was not chosen for the team. Aung Ngeain was. It was a potentially awkward situation, but Aung Ngeain's friend took it well.

"I felt really sad for her, but my friend was not jealous, she supported me," she says. "She said: 'Be a successful archery woman for me.'"

A similar message came from Aung Ngeain's father, although her mother was worried for her.

"My father said, if you are going to be successful, then go and do it. You have to prove you can be successful. If you're not going to succeed, don't go into this field. But my mum did not want me to become an archer," says Aung Ngeain. "She thought that as a girl, going to live in a difficult city would be hard, and was not safe for me."

Remember, in Myanmar, young women rarely live apart from their families. So when Aung Ngeain was plucked from her family home and state, and taken to the bustling commercial capital of Yangon, it was a huge thing for her and for her parents.

It was such a huge thing, in fact, that you get the impression that everyone involved thought it was an all-or-nothing game; or, as Aung Ngeain's father put it, she simply had to succeed. And while they were fearful for her, she says both her parents believed in her in a way she did not believe in herself.

"I never thought in my life that I would play in the sports field, that I would be an archer," she says. "When I was young, I did not have any ambition. Because we were poor, I just wanted to make money and support my family."

It was hard at first. In Yangon, the seventeen-year-old Aung Ngeain lived with other hopefuls in a sort of training camp, and she missed her family badly. She couldn't even call them, because of the lack of phones. She was far from the best archer there, too, she says.

"They selected four people from Chin state to train in Yangon. The trainer did not believe in me — I was not the best one. They always thought the others were better," she says.

But Aung Ngeain remembered what her dad had said, and she was determined to succeed. The training was intense but ultimately transformative. Four years later, Aung Ngeain won her first archery gold medal aged twenty-one. In fact, she won two.

"I got one gold medal when competing with the Southeast Asian nations, and the other was the ASEAN Games," says Aung Ngeain, matter-of-factly.

It was an amazing achievement: four years on from first picking up a bow, lacking the facilities and resources of many of the other nations in Asia that she was competing against, she triumphed.

As in many countries governed by repressive regimes, she hints at a slightly more threatening element to her training too, at least at the beginning, when Myanmar was still in the grip of the military junta.

She felt that competitors from other nations — who always appeared to her to be so relaxed — did not have the same pressure to make their nation seem great on the sporting field. There was an unspoken expectation on athletes like Aung Ngeain, to keep up appearances internationally when many global and regional powers had turned against the Burmese generals and their reign of terror.

"The government is like: 'You have to be successful for your own country.' There were many pressures," she says.

But she coped with them; although sadly, her mother was not there to see her success. She died after Aung Ngeain had been doing archery for two years, after suffering from a kind of brain seizure.

"It makes me so sad, because I wanted my mother to see me like this. She would be proud, she always wanted to see her daughter successful," says Aung Ngeain. "I always remember her when I am successful."

But while her family ties remain important to her, like many athletes the world over, she stresses how important it is to keep her emotions out of her sport.

"When I am shooting the arrow, I don't have anything in my mind," she says. It is this ability to focus, combined with Aung Ngeain's strength and determination, which have seen her become such a fearsome competitor on the international stage in the last decade.

"It takes only seconds to shoot an arrow," she says. "In those moments, I try not to think about anything. I try not to think about winning or losing. I don't think about my problems or happy memories. I just look at the target, and I shoot."

She meditates before she competes, and thinks of archery itself as meditative.

"It helps me to focus. Before a competition, in my mind, I picture myself shooting the arrow. In my mind, I play archery," she says.

And it is this mental element of archery which really appeals to her.

"I love archery because it is not all about the physical," she says. "It is a mixture of the mental and physical. I can use my brain in this sport. I like to say that archery is like meditation — it is good for your mind."

Aung Ngeain's father's words about success — the stern motivational mantra that if she was going to do it, she must succeed — also took her through training.

"I always remembered that, in training I remembered his voice and I used it as power. The first time I started to train I was not very good and I did not think I was going to be successful. But I kept going," she says.

She says one of her highlights was giving him one of her gold medals, in 2009, and later winning three gold medals in one competition — the only athlete to do so — at the SEA Games in 2011. She won for the solo competition and in the women's and mixed team events.

"When I heard I had got three gold medals, I was so shocked, I don't know how to describe it to you. There was so much going on in my mind — happy, sad, excited, everything. So many emotions," she says, beaming.

And her victory was also a victory for women in Myanmar. While Aung Ngeain says no one has ever explicitly told her that women can't shoot (and it would be a brave person that tried while she had bow and arrow in hand, I suspect), she has faced insidious discrimination for her entire career.

"Burmese people like male sports," she says. "When they hear about sports, they don't see women, they only see men."

She says more women need to take sport seriously in her country, despite the obstacles.

"Parents don't support their daughters to go into sports. It is hard and tiring, and they want their daughters to choose another field. Most of the women here think sport is so physical, it is not for them," she says.

But things are changing — in part thanks to Aung Ngeain herself.

"In the past people didn't know me, but now I get support. And when I get that I feel so happy. It is strength for me," she says.

She also feels that archery is uniquely suited for women who want to prove they are the equals of men, because the physical element is not as important. She trained with men, and prided herself on keeping up with them physically. But there's more to it than that.

"The mental side is so important in archery, and the men, they think they are better than women mentally as well. But I don't think so. I think I am equal to them," she says.

But despite the changes in attitude to her sport, and her own belief in herself, Aung Ngeain is still blunt in her assessment of the situation for women in Myanmar.

"There is no equality between men and women in this country," she says, shortly.

On the other hand, she has hope that her position as the country's most successful international archer has shown the men — and the women — of Myanmar a few things.

"I think people who think sport is not for women will see that I am successful, and because of me, girls want to be archers," she says.

And she has tough words for those who say girls can't do it.

"The people who say that kind of thing, they are outdated people. There should not be this discrimination against women — not only in sport, in any field. Nowadays we have seen women be successful in business, in sport, in lots of things. I think women need to be involved in everything — not only in sports, in everything."

In the sporting world, she is happy for now to be an inspiration for the girls who show up to her training classes in Naypyidaw. However, there are some obstacles that even she cannot yet overcome.

Aung Ngeain is married, and has a young son. She stopped competing in 2013 to focus on her family, despite being at the top of her game. She is obviously happy with her family, but the barriers that stop mothers from staying at the top of their game in Myanmar — and indeed in international sport globally — obviously rankle.

"I feel like I have wasted all my skills because I can't play archery anymore," she says. "I wasted all that time."

Like many working mothers, she regrets the fact that balancing her new role as a mother with her old role as an international sportswoman is hard.

"Life has become so much more difficult for me since I had my son. I can't play archery anymore, I don't have the time for training. I need to spend physical and mental strength only on my sport — I would not be able to look after my son," she says.

She wants to go back — in fact, the feeling is most acute when she watches her trainees in competition.

"I trained them really hard, but they were not what I expected. I wanted to go and be them. I wanted to shoot an arrow for them," she says.

Myanmar's archery community want her to go back too, but she says she won't return while she is still breastfeeding her child, who is only a one-year-old baby when we meet. When he is a bit older, maybe she will re-enter the competitive fray, she says — but to do so, she hopes her husband will step up to the unusual role in Myanmar of main caregiver, alongside a nanny.

After all, she says, her work in the world of sport is not over.

"People think men are good at sports, not women," she says. "And I had doubt in myself — can I do it? But then I started to train and I believed I could do it. I have proved a lot of things in my sport, so I am really happy about that."

But when my friend Thal Nyein Thu, who is translating the interview for me, teases Aung Ngeain that her pioneering role in female athleticism in Myanmar means she is like the Aung San Suu Kyi of sport (back in 2016, when this was still basically an uncomplicated compliment), the formidable competitor merely laughs. She then responds with the humility typical of all of the women in this book.

"Maybe not," she says. "I am just doing my job."

Conclusion

At the beginning of this book, I talked about hope, and how the world's hope in Aung San Suu Kyi has all but died as her government oversees what has all the hallmarks of genocide against the Rohingya in Rakhine State.

But I also talked about how, for all her faults, it was a speech by Aung San Suu Kyi that first set me on the path of meeting the remarkable women whose stories you have just read.

"Democracy is belief in the people," she said, speaking at the rally I mentioned in the Preface, as the sun beat down on the crowds in the fevered last few days before the November 2015 election.

A few days later, I was in the throng outside the NLD's headquarters in Yangon as the election results came in.

This time, it was raining, proper big droplet, soak-you-to-the-skin rain, but the mood was jubilant. Many were wearing NLD red, and some had bandanas knotted around their heads. Everyone was singing, and some were crying with joy as they watched the results arrive in Myanmar's first openly contested election in decades.

One man looked at the sky behind us. "Rain?" he said in English. "No problem!"

But for me and my kit, it was a slight problem, so I headed off to find shelter for a few hours until the rain eased off. Actually, as I walked towards a nearby café, the rain only got more intense; really hammering it down as my friend and I nudged past the human chain of volunteers forming a protective barrier between the revellers and the traffic.

With hopeless umbrellas and flooded streets, trousers plastered to our thighs and flip-flops in hand (nearly washed away by the flood), we pushed open the café doorway.

There was a beauty salon upstairs where we thought we could possibly borrow towels. Walking meekly up the staircase, leaving little rivulets of rainwater cascading down behind us, we were seized and bundled into a side room.

Switching on the air-con to the highest setting (to heat us up and take away the moisture from — well, us), the beauticians grinned and gestured at hairdryers and towels.

They didn't speak much English and I hardly speak any Burmese, but the message was clear: get in here, you silly foreigners, and let us help you.

They stripped off our clothes and handed us purple smocks to wear instead. Brandishing the hairdryers, they directed them at our hair, our dripping legs, our clothes.

At that moment, the salon owner popped her head in and laughed at our protestations that they were doing too much, waving away any suggestion of payment, and directing two of the others to bring us tea.

"You were at the NLD rally?" she asked us, her face shining. "I was there earlier. It's amazing."

She was not wrong: I've never been in a more electrifying place than on that street in Yangon that day and that night, as the rain poured down and the crowd chanted Suu Kyi's name.

And while they chanted Suu Kyi's name and roared at every glimpse of her on the giant video screen at the front, the Lady herself didn't appear, apparently too exhausted (and perhaps wary) to address the crowds that night, before the official results were confirmed.

So the electricity — and yes, the hope — was all from the crowd. And for me, it was all from the friendly beauticians down the road too, who showed us such kindness in the downpour.

And once again, I thought about how it was in the people themselves rather than the icon that I had found the most humanity and hope in Myanmar.

So I set out to meet the twelve women you have just read about, and hear their amazing, hopeful, brave, frustrating, sad and inspiring stories.

I began by thinking these women would appear in the book in addition to Aung San Suu Kyi; the backing singers to her soloist, if you like. While I lived in Myanmar, the veneration of Suu Kyi was such that it was hard to imagine that they could be anything else.

But after meeting them, leaving the country and returning to the U.K., and seeing the headlines about the violence in Rakhine state ramp up from disturbances to ethnic cleansing to probable genocide, I feel differently.

Now, while many in Myanmar do still have hope in their leader, I find it hard to have any hope in Suu Kyi. Instead, for me — and perhaps I have at least slightly convinced you — I can find hope in the women in this book. As such, far from being the backing singers for Suu Kyi, they have become the alternative.

As I complete this book, and as you read it, these Other Ladies — their stories, their struggles, their sacrifices and their courage — represent the people in whom even their own flawed heroine, Suu Kyi, claimed to have placed her own hope and belief for the future.

Moreover, they represent the stories of the millions of other people in the country who are not just hoping that they can build a better, more democratic and more equal future for themselves; they are actively working to do so, in the face of many obstacles.

Their stories are now the stories of hope in the complicated wider narrative of Myanmar's transition.

About the Author

 Jennifer Rigby is an award-winning British journalist who lived and worked in Yangon, Myanmar in 2015 and 2016. During that time, she travelled extensively around the country, meeting the women — and men — of Myanmar and hearing their stories as part of her work there. She specializes in women's rights, social affairs and people stories, and her work has been published by *The Telegraph*, *The Independent*, the BBC, *Newsweek*, IRIN and Refinery29, among others. She was born in 1984 and grew up in the north of England with her parents and sister before attending Bristol and Cardiff universities and moving to London in the mid-2000s. After a stint working in the Czech Republic as well as in Myanmar, Jennifer now lives and works as a freelance journalist in London, U.K. She loves reading, her digital radio, breakfast, and open-water swimming. She is married to Reuters journalist David Doyle, whose photography is featured on the cover of this book, and they have a son, Daniel.